GLOBETROTTER
TRAVEL GUIDE

KENYA

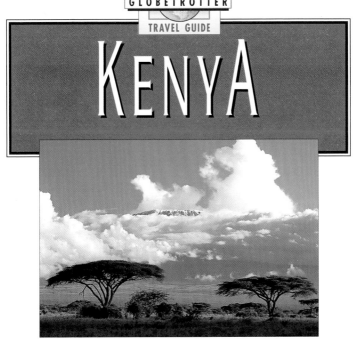

DAVE AND VAL RICHARDS

NEW
HOLLAND

GLOBETROTTER
TRAVEL GUIDE

First edition published in 1994 by
New Holland (Publishers) Ltd
London • Cape Town • Sydney

Copyright © 1994 in text: Dave and Val Richards
Copyright © 1994 in maps: Globetrotter
Travel Maps
Copyright © 1994 in photographs: Individual
photographers as credited right.
Copyright © 1994 New Holland (Publishers) Ltd

ISBN 1 85368 363 9

New Holland (Publishers) Ltd
Chapel House, 24 Nutford Place, London W1H 6DQ

Editor: Mariëlle Renssen
Indexer: Christine Riley
Design concept: Neville Poulter
Design and DTP: Mandy Moss
Cartography: Globetrotter Travel Maps
Typeset by Struik DTP
Reproduction by Hirt & Carter (Pty) Ltd, Cape Town
Printed and bound by Tien Wah Press (Pte) Ltd, Singapore

The authors would like to thank the following
people for their valuable assistance in the compiling
of this book: Tim and Nicky Tucker, Sol Rabb,
Sandra Faull, Fergus McCartney, Mike and
Elizabeth Mills, and the staff at Karen Connection.

Photographic credits: **Andrew Bannister** [STRUIK
IMAGE LIBRARY], cover (bottom left), pages 4, 7, 10
(right), 13, 15, 17 (right and left), 18, 21, 29, 31, 36, 39,
41, 42, 44, 53, 56, 57, 58, 60, 63, 64, 65, 66, 67, 68, 69,
70, 72, 73, 74, 75, 83, 85, 86, 88, 94, 95, 96, 97, 102, 105,
109, 111, 112, 116, 118, 119; **Daryl and Sharna
Balfour** [STRUIK IMAGE LIBRARY], cover (top
right and left, bottom right), title page, pages 6, 8, 16,
19, 23, 28, 32, 37, 38, 40, 45, 48, 71, 78, 81 (left and
right), 84, 87, 90, 93, 99, 110, 113, 114, 115; **David
Keith Jones**, page 35; **I Lichtenberg** [PHOTO
ACCESS], page 105 (left); **INPRA/Camera Press**,
page 22; **Patrick Wagner** [PHOTO ACCESS], pages
107, 117; **Dave Richards**, pages 10 (left), 11, 14, 20,
27, 43, 51, 52, 54, 55, 82, 98, 106; **David Steele**
[PHOTO ACCESS], page 30.

CONTENTS

1. INTRODUCTION
The Land
History in Brief
Government and Economy
The People

2. CENTRAL KENYA
Nairobi
Aberdare National Park
Mount Kenya National Park

3. WESTERN KENYA
Masai Mara National Reserve
Lake Victoria

4. GREAT RIFT VALLEY
Lake Turkana
Lake Baringo and Lake Bogoria
Lake Nakuru and Lake Naivasha

5. NORTHERN AND EASTERN KENYA
Samburu and Buffalo Springs
Shaba National Reserve
Meru National Park

6. SOUTHERN KENYA
Amboseli National Park
Tsavo National Park

7. CORAL COAST
Old Mombasa Town
South and North Coasts
Lamu Archipelago

TRAVEL TIPS

INDEX

1
Introducing
Kenya

Kenya covers an area slightly larger than France, and roughly the size of Texas in the United States. The equator almost exactly divides the country in half. With the Indian Ocean washing its eastern shores and the immense **Lake Victoria** on its western border, Kenya is truly a land of contrasts. From the snow-covered peaks of **Mount Kenya** astride the equator, to the warm sun-kissed beaches, the scenery embraces mountains, forests, deserts and lakes, plus a staggering diversity of wildlife.

Just as diverse is the proliferation of tribes and other peoples who have settled in this country, and the contrasts within Kenya's towns and cities: a good illustration is the contradiction between **Nairobi** and its modern high-rise buildings and traffic congestion, and **Lamu,** on the Indian Ocean, which still resembles an old Arab town and boasts only one motor car! Nairobi's infrastructure and its accessibility to many parts of the world make it an obvious first choice as a conference centre for many international organizations.

Most visitors are attracted to the country's coast, followed by its wonderful wildlife areas. Many come to climb **Mount Kenya**, and a smaller number is attracted by the deep-sea game-fishing, mainly around **Watamu** near **Malindi** on the north coast, and at **Shimoni** on the south coast near the Tanzanian border. Kenya also has many fine golf courses, with golfing safaris becoming a new tourist attraction. Visits to some of the national parks and reserves, as well as to the beaches, can easily be combined with a golfing vacation.

TOP ATTRACTIONS

*** Masai Mara National Reserve: Africa's finest wildlife area.
*** Coral Coast: unspoilt, sandy beaches, snorkelling and deep-sea fishing, ruins.
** Mount Kenya: climbing, walking, bird-watching and photographic opportunities.
** Tsavo West National Park: scenic, wildlife.
** Amboseli National Park: small, views of Kilimanjaro; elephant.
** Lake Nakuru: flocks of pink flamingo.

Opposite: *Diani Beach, on the south coast.*

FACTS AND FIGURES

Highest mountain is Mount Kenya at 5199m (17,058ft); although it lies on the equator, its summit and upper slopes are covered in snow and ice all year round.
Longest river is the Tana; it flows for almost 605km (376 miles) from the Mount Kenya and Aberdare slopes eastwards to the Indian Ocean, north of Malindi.
Largest waterfall is Gura Falls, around 457m (1500ft) high, in the Aberdare National Park.

Opposite: *the Mara River makes its serpentine way through the Masai Mara National Reserve.*
Below: *Lake Naivasha, in the Rift Valley.*

THE LAND

Kenya has several very distinct geographic regions. Two-thirds of the country, in the north and east, is mainly arid semidesert composed of acacia and commiphora bush, while the south and southwest comprise predominantly tree-dotted savanna at an altitude of between 900 and 1525m (3000 to 5000ft). In the east is a narrow fertile strip of land bordered by the Indian Ocean. Inland from this coastal stretch, the land quickly rises in altitude and soon becomes dry, inhospitable thorn-bush country. **Lake Victoria**, the world's second largest freshwater lake, lies to the west bordered by richly arable agricultural land.

Cutting through the country in a north–south direction is the **Great Rift Valley**, containing a string of lakes (most of which are strongly alkaline) and a number of mostly dormant volcanos. To the centre of Kenya, on the eastern edge of the Rift, an area of high plateau rises above 1829m (6000ft) and is dominated by **Mount Kenya**, the **Aberdare mountain range** and the Rift Valley. This area, aptly named the Highlands, is one of the world's richest agricultural areas. West of the Rift Valley in central Kenya lies the **Mau Escarpment**, another

high-lying rich farming area, which slowly falls away westwards down to Lake Victoria. To the north of the lake, on the border with Uganda, the second highest mountain within Kenya's boundary – one of the peaks of Mount Elgon's volcanic cone – rises to 4321m (14,177ft).

Mountains and Rivers

The upper slopes of the country's highest mountain, **Mount Kenya**, and its two adjacent salients make up the Mount Kenya National Park. The **Aberdare** mountain range, also a national park (the official new name of this park is Nyandarua but is hardly used), actually consists of two peaks, namely Ol Doinyo Satima and Kinangop. These are approximately 40km (25 miles) apart. Between these two peaks is a moorland plateau covered in coarse, tussocky grasses and giant heaths interspersed with forest patches.

To the west, the Kenya-Uganda border bisects **Mount Elgon**. The mountain slopes protruding into Kenya form a national park whose principal attractions are game-viewing, climbing and walking. There is also trout fishing. In the northeast of the country, the forested mountain of **Marsabit** rises out of a low, arid plain; it was made famous in the 1920s by the early game photographers, Martin and Osa Johnson, and more recently by Ahmed, an elephant sporting a spectacular pair of tusks and given presidential protection in 1970.

A number of mountain streams flowing from the slopes of Mount Kenya and the Aberdares converge to form the source of the **Tana**, Kenya's longest river. Most of the river's length traverses dry bush country, and

---

KENYA'S VISITORS

Visitors recorded in Kenya's national parks and reserves (1986):

Amboseli N.P.	157,000
Lake Nakuru N.P.	127,900
Masai Mara N.R.	94,800
Nairobi N.P.	91,600
Tsavo West N.P.	82,900
Tsavo East N.P.	75,300
Aberdares N.P.	42,500
Malindi Marine N.R.	36,100
Saiwa Swamp N.P.	1200

Most tourists are from Germany, Britain, Canada and the USA.

eventually discharges into the Indian Ocean south of Lamu. Both Meru and Kora national parks have their borders along the Tana. This river is also a major producer of hydroelectric power, supplying approximately 80% of Kenya's power; five hydroelectric dams exist along the Tana's banks.

The **Athi River** rises near Nairobi, and flows through the Tsavo East National Park and along the base of the **Yatta Plateau** on its way to the Indian Ocean. The 306km-long (190 miles) Yatta Plateau is one of the world's longest lava flows. After passing through Lugard's Falls (named after Lord Lugard who travelled up the river on his way to Uganda in 1890 where he was to become governor) in the Tsavo East National Park, the Athi changes its name to the **Galana** and turns eastwards, flowing through the park's arid thorn-bush country. As the Galana leaves Tsavo its name changes to **Sabaki**, which slowly meanders through riverine forest before meeting the Indian Ocean just north of the resort town of Malindi.

The **Mara River** rises in the Mau forest, flowing westwards through the Masai Mara National Reserve and on into the Serengeti National Park in Tanzania, from where it runs into Lake Victoria – source of the Nile. The **Saum-Turkwel** River has its source on Mount Elgon and heads northwards to Lake Turkana where Kenya's latest hydroelectric power plant in the Turkwel gorge has been completed. When operating to full capacity, it is expected to be Kenya's biggest producer of electrical power.

Seas and Shores

Lapped by the warm Indian Ocean, Kenya's coastline, from just north of Kiwaiyu on the Somalian border to Lunga Lunga on the Tanzanian border, boasts miles and miles of beautiful white beaches, interspersed with tidal creeks and mangrove swamps.

COMPARATIVE CLIMATE CHART	NAIROBI				LAKE NAKURU				MOMBASA			
	SUM JAN	AUT APR	WIN JULY	SPR OCT	SUM JAN	AUT APR	WIN JULY	SPR OCT	SUM JAN	AUT APR	WIN JULY	SPR OCT
MAX TEMP. °C	27	26	23	27	27	26	24	25	32	31	28	30
MIN TEMP. °C	13	15	11	13	8	11	10	9	23	24	21	22
MAX TEMP. °F	80	79	73	80	80	79	75	77	90	88	82	86
MIN TEMP. °F	55	59	52	55	46	52	50	48	73	75	70	72
HOURS SUN	9	6	4	7	9	6	7	6	8	7	7	9
RAINFALL in	2	6	.5	2	1	6	4	2	.5	4	1	2
RAINFALL mm	50	154	14	49	34	160	95	59	18	109	35	62

Opposite: running south from Mombasa is a string of enchanting lagoons, creeks and beaches and, here and there, relics of ancient Arab settlement.

Most of the tourist hotels are to be found to the north and south of Mombasa, Kenya's second largest city. Malindi, on the north coast, is also a major tourist centre. A wide variety of beach hotels line the shore from the pristinely modern to Arab-styled architecture blending perfectly into the local surroundings. Along the coast there are many remnants of old Arab civilizations that flourished 500 years ago, the best examples of which are the 15th-century ruins of the town of **Gedi**, just south of Malindi. Near to Gedi is **Mida Creek**, world famous in ornithological circles for its huge concentrations and variety of shore birds. The **Lamu Archipelago**, too, is steeped in history: tumbling ruins reflect the rich cultural influences from centuries of Arab-African civilization. On Manda Island the ruins of **Takwa** dating back to the 16th or 17th centuries, are as archaeologically significant as Gedi.

The coast's marine national reserves offer a rainbow-coloured array of fish and wonderful coral – a haven for snorkellers and scuba divers. Watamu and Malindi to the north are renowned for their exhilarating deep-sea fishing (sailfish, marlin, tunny).

Climate

As most of Kenya is high-plateau country it enjoys a pleasant climate: warm days and cool nights are the norm for most of the year. In the Highlands and Rift Valley it is not unusual to experience temperatures of around 30°C (86°F) during the day, while at night one can happily sit in front of a log fire, as the temperature drops below 10°C (50°F). Around Lake Victoria and at the coast, however, it can be very hot and humid, although the sea breezes off the Indian Ocean make a stay at the coast very pleasant.

For most of Kenya, the main rains normally occur during the period March to May, followed by a short rainy period towards the end of October, lasting until early December. However, there are local variations. Along the coastal strip the rains are mainly from May until July and again in November. In the areas around Lake Victoria, the lake itself has a strong influence on the weather and it can rain, usually at night, during every month of the year.

Above: *the pale pink springtime blooms of a Cape chestnut grace the Aberdare uplands. The species belongs to the citrus family.*

Above right: *a shy bushbuck, relative of the much larger kudu and invariably seen near water, pauses in the woodland fringes of Lake Nakuru.*

Opposite: *a typical landscape in the alpine heath zone.*

The amount of rainfall varies considerably across the country: western Kenya receives from 1016 to 1270mm (40 to 50in) a year; the central highlands and Rift Valley, 762 to 1016mm (30 to 40in); while the northern and eastern areas are lucky if they receive 254mm (10in) a year.

Plant Life

The country's coastal strip, although only a few miles wide, has a rich and varied vegetation: mangroves grow in the tidal bays and creeks, and mangrove poles are an important export commodity. Along the coastline coconut palms, cashew-nut trees and sisal plantations dominate.

Remnants of the once-extensive coastal forest still remain (the **Arabuko-Sokoke** near Malindi has been proclaimed a forest reserve thus protecting this rapidly dwindling indigenous tract).

The coast's fertile land quickly gives way to dry woodland and then to arid bush country, which covers almost two-thirds of Kenya. Extensive montane forests remain in the central highlands, surrounded by rich agricultural land where wheat, maize, coffee and other crops are cultivated. Further west, in the highland bordering Lake Victoria, the major tea-growing area is centred on the town of Kericho. On Lake Victoria's shore to the north of Kisumu, **Kakamega Forest** is a remnant of the once-great rainforest that stretched from Africa's west coast to its east.

Of special interest within Kenya's diverse vegetation zones is the highest-occurring one on the country's mountain slopes – the alpine heath zone. Three distinctive vegetation belts ring Kenya's mountains: grassland, forest and finally the weird and wonderful alpine sector.

The forest zone follows the grasslands at around 2440m (800ft) and consists of bamboo and giant *Podocarpus* species (yellowwoods); this slowly gives way to leafy forests of twisted lianas and hagenia trees draped with orchids and Spanish moss, also known as 'old man's beard'. At the upper limit of this zone –

around 3050m (10,000ft) – giant St John's wort (*Hypericum* sp.) with its bright yellow flowers begins to appear. Open areas of tussock grass featuring giant heaths (*Erica arborea*) also hung with strands of old man's beard now occur. Growing amidst the coarse grasses are everlasting flowers (*Helichrysum* sp.), turquoise delphiniums, and proteas – one of which produces a spiky yellow flower that resembles cat's claws, and is thus often referred to as 'lion claws'. Higher up are the fascinating giant lobelias and groundsels with, in the wetter areas, red-hot pokers and fiery gladioli.

At these high altitudes the climate is severe, with hot, summer conditions during the day and icy winter temperatures at night.

> **DISAPPEARING FOREST**
>
> Kenya is having a difficult time conserving her forests. Certain trees are required for the timber trade, but the forests are also under pressure from the human population, which is cutting down trees to make way for the planting of crops. Forests occurring within national parks are well protected. The unique Kakamega Forest is only partially protected; a small part is national park area with the rest a reserve that is constantly under threat: a few years ago part of the forest was cleared for the growing of tea.

Wild Kingdom

Kenya's wildlife heritage is for many people its prime
attraction. The best-known wildlife areas are **Amboseli
National Park**, which is dominated by the snow-covered
Mount Kilimanjaro, and the **Masai Mara National
Reserve**, famous for its abundance of game and its many
predators. Other impressive wildlife areas are the three
national reserves to the northeast, set in arid bush country along the banks of the area's only river, the Ewaso
Nyiro: they are **Samburu**, **Buffalo Springs** and **Shaba**.
These reserves are notable for the unusual species they
contain: the endangered Grevy's zebra, herds of beisa
oryx, the long-necked gerenuk and the very striking
reticulated giraffe.

To the south and east of the country lie **Tsavo East**
and **Tsavo West** national parks which are bisected by
the main Nairobi–Mombasa highway. Together, the
parks form one of the largest wildlife areas in the entire

Opposite: *a lioness at rest
in the Masai Mara reserve,
part of the famed Serengeti
ecosystem. For three or four
months each year the
annual migration brings
more than two million
large herbivores onto the
Mara grasslands, and the
predators flourish.*

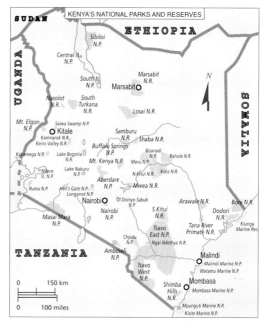

KENYA'S NATIONAL PARKS AND RESERVES

world – 20,812km^2 (8035 sq miles) – in contrast to the tiny **Saiwa Swamp National Park** which is only 2km^2 (half a square mile) in size, and is possibly the world's smallest national park. Another park deserving a mention is **Lake Nakuru**, famous for its spectacular flamingos: sometimes as many as 1.5 million make their home there.

Kenya's numerous and varied birdlife (1075 species) is attracting increasing numbers of ornithologists and bird-watchers, and is the fastest growing sector of the tourist industry. Sixty-six different birds of prey have been recorded (excluding owls); among these are 19 eagles, from the mighty martial to the tiny pygmy falcon. Eight species of vulture are found in Kenya, namely the palm nut, African white-backed, Rüppell's, hooded, Egyptian, lappet-faced and white-headed species, and finally, the rarest, the lammergeyer.

Conserving Kenya's Natural Heritage

Like every other African country, Kenya's wildlife areas, forests and special habitats are continuously being threatened, mostly by an expanding population's need for more land, by increasing urbanization and industrial

---

WHERE TO SPOT THE BIG FIVE

• Lion: a nocturnal hunter, but easiest cat to see in the Masai Mara during the day.
• Leopard: shy and nocturnal, it can however usually be seen in the Masai Mara, Samburu and Lake Nakuru reserves on early morning and late afternoon drives.
• Elephant: seen in most wildlife areas (except Nairobi and Saiwa Swamp parks); best place is Amboseli, around swamps at midday.
• Buffalo: most dangerous of Africa's animals, can best be seen in the Masai Mara and Aberdare national parks.
• Rhino: both black and white species, most confined to protected areas; see them in Nairobi, Nakuru and Aberdare parks; Solio Ranch and Lewa Conservancy.

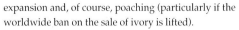

expansion and, of course, poaching (particularly if the worldwide ban on the sale of ivory is lifted).

But there have been signs of hope. Since Dr Richard Leakey and the Kenya Wildlife Service took over the running of the national parks (philosopher Dr David Western replaced Dr Leakey in early 1994), there has been a dramatic drop in poaching; rhino have not been poached for over two years. Entry fees for the national parks have been raised substantially and a proportion of this now goes directly to the people living adjacent to these wildlife reserves. The money is used to help the local people build health clinics, schools and improve the roads. There are plans to fence the parks (at the time of writing, work had started on the Aberdare National Park). This has proved to be very popular with the local people as the fencing stops the wildlife from raiding their *shambas* (small farms).

The East African Wildlife Society raises large sums of money to fund various wildlife research programmes. Also strongly active, and perhaps most important of all, the organization Wildlife Clubs of Kenya teaches the citizens of tomorrow the importance of conservation. Many national parks now have educational facilities, exhibits and interpretation centres. The Nairobi National Park has a very active education centre where groups of schoolchildren can experience wildlife conservation lectures and film shows.

Birding Hot Spots

Kakamega Forest: a visit to this forest is a must for every keen bird-watcher; many bird species not normally found elsewhere

Below: *the colourful Hartlaub's turaco.*

in Kenya can be spotted here (blue-headed bee-eater, yellow-billed barbet, brown-eared woodpecker, dusky tit, Cameroon sombre greenbul and yellow-bellied wattle-eye).

Lake Baringo: over 400 species have been recorded here; not to be missed is an early morning walk with Lake Baringo Club's resident ornithologist and a boat trip along the lake shore (Verreaux's eagle, Goliath heron, Hemprich's and Jackson's hornbill).

Above: *a bevy of vulturine guineafowl makes its way through the Samburu scrub north of Mount Kenya.*

Samburu-Buffalo Springs reserves: many species found only in the north and east of Kenya can be seen here (pygmy falcon, Somali bee-eater, buff-crested bustard, vulturine guineafowl, magpie starling and the localized Donaldson Smith's sparrow weaver).

Mount Kenya: Naro Moru River Lodge, at the base of Mount Kenya, is a bird-watcher's dream; it is not uncommon to see 10 different sunbird species on one visit to the area (the tacazze sunbird is the highlight). Other birds to be spotted include African black duck, emerald cuckoo, red-headed parrot, giant kingfisher, Hartlaub's turaco, cinnamon-chested bee-eater, mountain wagtail and white-starred forest robin.

Mountain Lodge: in addition to the birds listed for the Naro Moru River Lodge, this night game-viewing spot on the slopes of Mount Kenya has Doherty's bush shrike, grey-headed Negro finch and Abyssinian crimsonwing.

Other places are **Lake Nakuru** for flamingos and shorebirds, **Lake Naivasha** for a variety of waterbirds and **Masai Mara** for vultures, eagles and other birds of prey; **Arabuko-Sokoke** conceals the world's rarest owl, the Sokoke scops owl.

SUNBIRDS

Sunbirds, like the humming birds of the Americas, feed mostly on nectar taken from flowers. Of Africa's 70 species, 35 are resident in Kenya. It is possible to see 10 different sunbirds in a day at Naro Moru River Lodge. The birds are characterized by their thin, curved bills and the bright, colourful plumage of the males. When feeding on nectar, pollen from the flower brushes off onto the sunbird's forehead and as the bird visits other flowers, is transferred from one blossom to another. This method of pollination is an extremely important exchange between bird and flower.

Above: Maasai family members outside their home.

HISTORY IN BRIEF

As new evidence comes to light, the theory that East Africa – or Kenya, for that matter – is the cradle of mankind is gaining strength among scientists. Believed to be the first signs of ancient man in Kenya is the collection of stone tools found – and later some 400 hominid fossils – by anthropologist-palaeontologist Dr Richard Leakey at the desolate **Koobi Fora** excavation site on the eastern shores of Lake Turkana. One particular skull is dated 2.5 million years ago.

The first indigenous people to wander across Kenya in search of food were hunter-gatherers who were later forced out or assimilated by later arriving people. **Kikuyu** legend weaves stories around pygmies who, they recounted, lived in the forests to which the Kikuyu were slowly migrating. The **Ndorobo** people, a small tribe who still hunt with bows and arrows, and gather honey in traditional ways, are very likely descendants of these early people.

As a result of migrations from north Africa around 3500 years ago, the region was slowly being settled by people of three different origins, classified mainly by the language they spoke: the Cushitic, Nilotic and Bantu peoples. The Cushites were nomadic pastoralists moving down from Ethiopia, while the Nilotic tribe, also pastoralists, originated from the Nile valley (the Southern Nilotes settled in the Lake Turkana area and are the ancestors of the present Turkana and Maasai peoples). The Bantu people were iron-makers and agriculturalists (which they still are today), and they form the vast majority of present-day Kenyans. Unfortunately, little is known of these tribal movements as no written records appear to have been kept.

KENYA'S INDIGENOUS PEOPLES

• The **Bantu** tribe is made up of two groups: eastern and western. The eastern group is composed of the Kikuyu, Embu, Meru and Kamba, while the western comprises the Abaluyia and the Kisii.

• The **Nilotic** people are split into three groups: the highland group, which includes the Kipsigis, Nandi and Tugen; the plains group represented by the well-known Maasai and the Samburu; and the lake group, the Luo, who probably moved into present-day Kenya as recently as 400 years ago from the southern Sudan.

• The Somalis make up the majority of the **Cushitic** peoples.

• Other groups are the Galla and the Rendille.

The Birth of Swahili

The arrival of Islam on the coast around the 9th century through the interaction of passing traders left a rich cultural and architectural legacy. Between the 10th and 15th centuries, as a result of the large trade network that covered the Indian Ocean, a series of cities and towns was established along the East African coast, from Somalia in the north to Mozambique in the south. The history of this settlement by Arab and Persian peoples was recorded in Kiswahili (a name derived from the Arabic word *sahel*, for 'coast'). Eventually, the architects of these cities integrated with the coastal Africans creating an Arab-African culture that today is known as Swahili.

In 1498 Vasco da Gama, the Portuguese sailor-explorer, called at Mombasa to pick up a navigator who would guide him to India (his arrival was not welcomed by the Arabs and he was forced to sail on to Malindi). Da Gama's travels paved the way for other adventurers to explore the East African coast. Following on from this, the coastal peoples were increasingly subjected to

> **GALLA TRIBE**
>
> The Galla people originated from southern Ethiopia. Galla means 'wandering'; they are indeed highly mobile, constantly in search of water and grazing for their herds, which include camels. Their simple, dome-shaped huts are made from doum palm leaves, woven into mats, and laid onto pliable saplings, which are placed in a circle in the ground and tied together in the centre. They now live in the area around the Tana River in Eastern Kenya.

Below left: *Lamu's market-place, next to the Old Fort.*
Below: *one of Lamu's beautifully carved doors.*

THOMSON'S EXPEDITION

Joseph Thomson's Rift Valley explorations proved of some importance; it was he who named the Aberdares (after Lord Aberdare, president of the Royal Geographical Society), a mountain range rising above the Kinangop Plateau, which he climbed while at Lake Naivasha. Passing around the northern edge of the Aberdares and on to the Laikipia Plateau, he saw Mount Kenya, so confirming Krapf's discovery. He also came across a waterfall in this region, which was named Thomson's Falls after him (now renamed Nyahururu). Next, he walked to Lake Baringo, where he spent some time mapping the area. He then headed westwards, crossing the Kerio Valley, the Uasin Gishu Plateau and finally reaching Lake Victoria, where he made the decision to turn back.

pressure throughout the 16th and 17th centuries, not only from the Portuguese but also from the fierce Galla warriors, a migratory nomadic people originating from Ethiopia.

The Portuguese eventually captured Mombasa in 1505 and in 1593, they commenced building Fort Jesus; here they held sway until 1698 when the fort was captured by Sayyid Said, the Sultan of Oman and Zanzibar. During Portuguese rule there had been little contact with inland tribes because of hostility and fear, which was effective in keeping Kenya largely free of the slave trade that was well underway during that period.

First European Explorers

The first Europeans to explore Kenya were probably **F.L. Krapf** and **F. Rebmann**, two German missionaries working on behalf of the Church Missionary Society. In 1847 Rebmann explored inland as far as the Taita Hills. In the following year, on 11 May, Rebmann became the first European to record having seen the snow- and ice-covered Mount Kilimanjaro. In 1849 Krapf saw Kilimanjaro for the first time, and later, from a hill near Kitui, he sighted Mount Kenya. Then in 1882 a German doctor, **Gustav Fischer**, who was embarking on a scientific collecting expedition, entered Kenya along the Rift Valley from Tanzania and eventually walked as far north

Opposite: *a close wildlife encounter, with Mount Kilimanjaro providing a magnificent backdrop.*
Right: *flamingos congregate at Lake Bogoria in the Baringo district of the Rift Valley. Europeans first explored the area in the 1880s, when Joseph Thomson led a Royal Geographical Society expedition to Lake Victoria.*

as Naivasha. On his way back to the coast he passed through Hell's Gate, where his name is still remembered in the form of a column of rock called Fischer's Column.

The next explorer was **Joseph Thomson**, who led a Royal Geographic Society expedition in 1883. From the coast he walked through what is now Amboseli National Park and on to Ngong, near present-day Nairobi, which was then a stopping-off point on the edge of the Rift Valley for ivory caravans. From Ngong he descended into the Rift Valley, which he penetrated as far north as Lake Baringo. Here, he cut westwards to Lake Victoria, where he then decided to turn back. Thomson stopped off first to visit the now famous Elephant Caves on Mount Elgon, then made his way to Lakes Baringo, Nakuru and Naivasha, before finally returning to Mombasa.

The next European explorer to pass this way was **James Hannington** who had been appointed Bishop of Buganda (in present-day Uganda). Hannington discovered a lake that Joseph Thomson had missed, which was later named Lake Hannington (now known as Lake Bogoria) in his honour. Hannington was later murdered when he arrived at the Nile.

Count Samuel Teleki von Szek and his companion **Lieutenant Ludwig von Höhnel** were the next explorers to follow Thomson's route and in 1887 arrived at the foot of Mount Kenya, which Teleki tried unsuccessfully to climb. They then went on to Lake Baringo and continued northwards to discover a new lake, which they named Lake Rudolf, after the crown prince of Austria. The following year in 1889, **Frederick Jackson**, who later became Sir Frederick Jackson and the first governor of the Colony of Kenya, led an expedition sponsored by the Imperial British East Africa Company to explore the territories it had been granted.

Above: *one of the grand old steam work-horses on display in Nairobi's evocative Railway Museum.*

THE LUNATIC LINE

In order to build the Uganda Railway – dubbed the 'Lunatic Line' by poet Henry Labouchère – thousands of workers were brought over from India (mainly Punjabis who were of the Sikh religion) owing to the problems experienced with recruiting local tribespeople to do the heavy work. During construction, hundreds of these Indian workers died of disease, malaria being the main culprit, and at least 28 were killed by lion. Heavy rains washed away miles of embankment; excessive heat was a big problem in the Taru Desert area, while bitterly cold weather, ice and sleet had to be endured at the Mau summit.

Formation of the Imperial British East Africa Company

Meanwhile, during this time of exploration, the scramble for Africa had begun. In 1877 the Sultan of Zanzibar offered William MacKinnon (later 'Sir') of the British East Africa Association a concession to administer mainland East Africa as his vassal; the offer was not accepted. In 1885, at the Berlin Conference attended by 13 European nations and the USA, it was decided that the Sultan's rule did not extend beyond the 10-mile strip along the East African coast. The Sultan again offered the mainland to the British East Africa Association in 1887; this time it was accepted, with the power to exercise full judicial and political authority and to levy customs duties. The company was granted a Royal Charter in April 1888 and renamed the Imperial British East Africa Company.

In 1890 the Anglo-German Agreement was signed, giving interior Tanganyika to the Germans, and the whole of Uganda and interior Kenya to Britain. Uganda became a British protectorate in 1894; it was considered to have great potential, and more importantly, it would enable Britain to control the source of the River Nile. Uganda covered a much larger area at this time: its eastern areas included much of modern western Kenya, stretching as far east as Naivasha in the Rift Valley.

The Building of the Uganda Railway

Early in 1885 the British Parliament decided to build a railway 965km (600 miles) long from Mombasa to Kisumu (then part of Uganda). Also in the same year, Britain took over the administration of the Imperial British East Africa Company and the 16km (10 miles) coastal strip on behalf of the Sultan of Zanzibar. As a result, all the land from the coast to the Ugandan border

Left: *Kikuyu in ceremonial mode. Largest of Kenya's ethnic groups, the Kikuyu began farming in the fertile area south of Mount Kenya some 400 years ago, later coming into conflict with European settlers in quest of good land.*

became a protectorate known as the British East African Protectorate. The building of the Uganda Railway was a mammoth task, costing the British Government £5 million – a lot of money in those days. Work was started in 1895, the first rail laid in 1896, and it took four years to reach what's now Nairobi, finally reaching Kisumu in 1901.

The railway not only ensured better access to Uganda but also opened up Kenya to the early settlers. It was about this time that Lord Delamere settled in the Rift Valley on a 40,500ha (98,840 acres) ranch near Nakuru. Over the years, despite Delamere's decreasing wealth and after failures and setbacks, he proved that the Highlands were fertile and very suitable for settlement.

In 1902 the border between Uganda and Kenya was adjusted to its present position, leaving the Uganda railway firmly in Kenya. It was not until 1931 that the railway eventually reached Kampala, Uganda's capital.

Kenya became a protectorate in 1905, when its administration was transferred from the Foreign Office to the Colonial Office and then became the East African Protectorate.

After World War I there was a big influx of European settlers; unfortunately most knew little of farming; farms were either given away to lottery winners or sold at a nominal cost on long-term credit.

Rumblings of Discontent

In 1920, the status of Kenya was changed from a protectorate to a crown colony, except for the coastal strip which remained a protectorate under lease from the Sultan of Zanzibar. At this time the settler population was about 9000, and it appeared that Kenya was on its way to becoming a permanent 'white man's country'. But there were also signs of African disenchantment. In 1921, the Young Kikuyu Association was formed by Henry Thuku, a telephone operator at the treasury; in the following year, the association drew up a petition containing a number of grievances concerning land, and

JOMO KENYATTA

A Kikuyu, Jomo Kenyatta wasborn in 1882, north of Nairobi; educated at mission school, at 29 joined Nairobi Municipal Council as water-meter inspector; became involved in politics, changed name to Jomo Kenyatta, went into self-imposed exile in England in 1931; returned to Kenya in 1946, elected head of KAU a year later; arrested October 1952 by colonial government and incarcerated; while in jail, elected president of KANU; released Aug 1961, in Nov led delegation of KANU delegates to London to discuss Kenya's future; first general elections held May 1963; Kenyatta elected MP for Gahundu; Kenya granted internal self-government 1 Jun, Kenyatta first prime minister. Independence on 12 Dec 1964, Kenyatta became first president, succeeded by Daniel arap Moi in August 1978.

the carrying of a *kipande*, or registration card. The petition led to Harry Thuku's arrest. A crowd gathered outside the Central Police Station where he was being held, shots were fired and at least 23 Africans were killed or died later of their injuries. Thuku was later deported.

The settlers suffered a further setback when a British Government White Paper revived the old policy of 'Africa for the Africans'. Called the Devonshire White Paper, it stated: 'Kenya is an African territory … the interests of the African native must be paramount, and that if and when those interests and the interests of the immigrant races should conflict, then the former should prevail.' In the same year Mzee Jomo Kenyatta became a member of the committee of the East Africa Association (Mzee, a term given to Kenyatta by his people, is one of respect meaning 'father' or 'elder').

There was much discontent among the settler population, and there was even talk of rebellion, but as their numbers were never significant enough, the talk soon fizzled. In 1925, due to pressure, the name of the East Africa Association was changed to the Kikuyu Central Association; in 1928 Mzee Kenyatta became its secretary and started the Kikuyu newspaper *Mwigwithania* (the reconciler). The following year Kenyatta went to England to make personal representation to the British

Government about Kikuyu grievances and in 1930, before returning to Kenya, he published their injustices and demands in the British press. He returned to Britain in 1931 to continue his work, and Harry Thuku was released from detention. In 1932 tribal reserves were established, to be administered along tribal lines – Maasailand is an example. In the same year, Jomo Kenyatta returned to England to give evidence before the Carter Commission.

During 1940 the Kikuyu Central Association, the Ukamba Members Association and the Taita Hills

Opposite: *Jomo Kenyatta (left), father of modern Kenya, and Dr Jonas Savimbi of UNITA.*
Left: *the 24m (79ft) monument in the Uhuru Gardens, on the way to Nairobi National Park, where Kenya finally gained its freedom from colonial rule. Surrounding the monument are lush grounds laid out within a 'map' of the country.*

Association were banned and their leaders arrested. However in 1944, the first African, Mr Eliud Mathu, was nominated to the Legislative Council, replacing two Europeans overseeing African interests. Late in 1946 Kenyatta returned to Kenya and in the following year replaced James Gichuru as president of the Kenya Africa Union (KAU), previously known as the Kenya African Study Union.

Mau Mau Uprising

During 1948 the first stirrings of the Mau Mau freedom fight began, and in 1952 Jomo Kenyatta together with five of his comrades were arrested; on 20 October, a State of Emergency was declared.

Armies of freedom fighters made up mostly of Kikuyu moved into the forests of Mount Kenya and the Aberdares to wage guerrilla warfare on the European population. This rebellion lasted until 1957, but the emergency was not declared over until 1960. During this time, changes were taking place. In 1957 eight African members were elected to the Legislative Council, and in 1959 a turning point in African representation on the Council occurred when 25 African members were elected with 15 Asians, 5 Arabs and 46 Europeans. African membership continued to rise and non-African membership fell.

MAU MAU

The Kikuyu settled around Mt Kenya, the Aberdares and north of Nairobi. These areas also attracted European settlers. Trouble started with the slaughter of a European farmer's cattle in 1953, followed by the killing of a number of Kikuyus for their loyalty to the colonial government. The rebellion became known as Mau Mau; other tribes were also involved – mostly Luo and Maasai. The rebellion was only put down with the help of the British army in 1956.

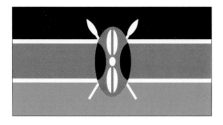

Above: *Kenya's national flag was formally raised for the first time, in Nairobi's Uhuru Gardens, on 12 December 1963.*

Freedom at Last

In March 1960 the Kenya African National Union (KANU) was formed and in May, while Mzee Jomo Kenyatta was still being held in prison, he was elected its president. This was followed by the formation of the Kenya African Democratic Union (KADU). The State of Emergency ended.

In February 1961 the general elections, in which Africans participated for the first time, resulted in a KANU victory with 67% of the vote against KADU's 16%. In August, Kenyatta was released from detention and in November led a delegation to England.

The year 1963 was the climax of the struggle for freedom. On 1 June, internal self-government (*Jamhuri*) was proclaimed with KANU forming the government and Jomo Kenyatta the first prime minister. During Kenyatta's inaugural speech, he gave Kenya the national motto *Harambee*, meaning 'let's all pull together'. In August Kenyatta addressed European settlers in Nakuru, convincing them to stay and contribute to an independent Kenya.

At midnight of 12 December, Kenya obtained its Independence: Uhuru, or freedom. In a colourful historic ceremony, attended by Prince Philip representing the Queen, the Union Jack was lowered for the last time and the black, red and green flag of Kenya raised.

A year later Kenya became a republic with Jomo Kenyatta as its first president. Kenyatta led the country along a moderate path, preached reconciliation with the European population and tolerence towards the Asian community, encouraging foreign investment and close links with the West.

On 22 August 1978, Mzee Kenyatta died at his Mombasa home. Nominated by KANU on 6 October 1978 as the sole candidate for president, then vice-president Daniel Toroitich arap Moi succeeded Jomo Kenyatta in an orderly fashion. President Moi's new national slogan is *Nyayo*, 'to follow in the footsteps'.

DANIEL ARAP MOI

Born in 1924 in Baringo district; was a school teacher before entering politics in 1955 when elected member of Legislative Council for Rift Valley; became Kenya's third vice-president in Jan 1967; after Kenyatta's death automatically elected new president; major achievements include introduction of free education and free milk for all primary school students, and doubling of number of primary schools; in 1981 elected chairman of the OAU (Organization of African Unity), a position held for an unprecedented two terms.

HISTORICAL CALENDAR

900-1499 Arab/Africa civilization flourishes on east coast.
1498 Vasco da Gama sails to Mombasa.
1593 Portuguese start building Fort Jesus at Mombasa.
1698 Army of Sultan of Oman and Zanzibar captures Fort Jesus from Portuguese.
1848–49 First European sightings of Mount Kilimanjaro and Mount Kenya.
1877 Sultan of Zanzibar offers British East Africa Association concession to administer mainland East Africa.
1883 Joseph Thomson's expedition up Rift Valley.
1888 Sir Frederick Jackson's exploration of Kenya.
1895-1901 Construction of Uganda Railway; reaches Lake Victoria at Port Florence (now Kisumu).
1902 Uganda-Kenya border readjusted to present position.

1908 Kenya becomes East African Protectorate.
1920 Kenya becomes a crown colony.
1929 Kenyatta visits England to air Kikuyu grievances.
1944 First African elected to Legislative Council.
1948 Mau Mau uprising.
1952 State of Emergency.
1959 25 Africans elected to Legislative Council.
1960 Political parties KANU and KADU formed.
1963 Internal self-government granted on 1 Jun, followed by full Independence on 12 Dec; Kenyatta first prime minister.
1964 Kenya a republic 12 Dec, Kenyatta first president.
1974 Swahili becomes official language of Parliament.
1976 Idi Amin, Uganda's president, claims large portions of Sudan and Kenya.
1977 Hunting banned.

1978 President Jomo Kenyatta dies; Daniel arap Moi sworn in as new president.
1979 President Moi decrees that all rhino in Kenya be protected.
1982 Attempted coup by Kenya Air Force.
1989 Dr Richard Leakey made director of Department of Wildlife; President Moi burns 12 tons of ivory in public ceremony in Nairobi National Park.
1991 Constitution amended, opening way for registration of opposition parties.
1992 First multiparty elections held in Dec.
1993 Kenya hit by serious drought and ethnic clashes in Rift Valley.
1994 Dr Richard Leakey resigns as director of Kenya Wildlife Service. President Moi appoints Dr David Western as new director.

GOVERNMENT AND ECONOMY

Kenya is a republic within the Commonwealth with the president, as commander-in-chief of the Armed Forces, heading the National Assembly, which forms the Legislature. The president must be a member of the National Assembly and is normally elected through a general election process, which follows the dissolution of Parliament. The vice-president and the Cabinet are appointed by the president and must also be members of the Assembly. Elections for both the president and the National Assembly are held every five years.

Since 1969 Kenya has been a one-party state. In November 1991, however, Kenya reverted to a multiparty state. For administration purposes, Kenya is divided into eight provinces (of which Nairobi is one), each headed by a provincial commissioner. These eight provinces are divided into 41 districts, each administered by a district commissioner.

COMPOSITION OF NATIONAL ASSEMBLY

The National Assembly consists of a single chamber with 188 elected members, 12 nominated members, a speaker and an attorney general. The speaker is elected by the National Assembly; the attorney general is usually a civil servant appointed by the president. Candidates for a national election, unless nominated unopposed, are selected at a Party preliminary election. The government has 28 ministries, each headed by a minister and two assistant ministers, and administered by a permanent secretary.

Kenya's Wealth

Kenya is one of the most prosperous African nations, with a record of stability and sound government since Independence. Despite the fact that only 18% of the country's land is fertile and has cultivation potential, the economy is firmly based on agriculture which accounts for two-thirds of the country's exports. This is backed by tourism, manufacturing and commerce. Kenya is the third largest tea producer in the world, the largest producer of pyrethrum (a natural insecticide) and a major exporter of coffee, cut flowers and vegetables.

Tourism continues to be a major source of revenue and employment despite a levelling off in the number of visitors – mainly due to the recession in Europe and the United States, negative publicity in the overseas press, and rising travel costs. Most visitors are from Germany, followed by Britain, the USA and Switzerland. In 1991 earnings from tourism were US$1904 million from 804,600 visitors.

Kenya has a strong manufacturing sector, producing many consumer products that were once imported. A number of motor-vehicle assembly plants supply both a local and an export market. Last, but certainly not least, is the *Jua-kali* sector, the name given to the roadside businesses that are such a common feature these days in the towns and villages of Kenya.These businesses provide essential employment opportunities and produce cheap manufactured goods, mostly from scrap, roadside garage facilities and other items for the lower-income people. *Jua-kali* means 'hot sun', as the workers operate outside in the blazing heat.

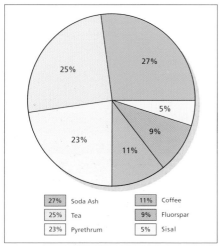

KENYA'S MAJOR EXPORTS

27%	Soda Ash	11%	Coffee
25%	Tea	9%	Fluorspar
23%	Pyrethrum	5%	Sisal

Infrastructure

The port of Mombasa is the major gateway for East Africa, serving not only Kenya but also Uganda, Rwanda, Burundi, eastern Zaïre, southern Sudan, and also northern Tanzania. The port has 18 berths, two bulk oil jetties and a container terminal.

The Kenya Railways system provides 2085km (1295 miles) of railway line for both passenger and freight services. The passenger network runs from Nairobi to Mombasa, Nairobi to Kisumu, and Nairobi to Kampala in Uganda. Several branch lines are for freight only.

Kenya Airways, the national carrier, has a well-developed international and domestic network, and owns a modern fleet of aircraft (Airbus A300s, Boeing 737s and Fokker F50s). There are two international airports, Nairobi's **Jomo Kenyatta** and Mombasa's **Moi International**. In addition, there are over 150 local airports and airstrips, served by both Kenya Airways and a number of private-schedule and charter airlines. Among these airlines are Air Kenya, Africair, Safari Air and Prestige Air Services.

Of Kenya's 63,000km (39,148 miles) of roads, 13% are bitumen-surfaced. Over half of all freight traffic is transported by road, especially to Kenya's neighbouring countries. Public transport is mainly by country bus or by taxis known as matatus (*see* panel). Unfortunately, Kenya's accident rate is extremely high.

> **MATATUS**
>
> Matatus are privately owned taxis; originally small cars such as Peugeot 404s, they are now predominantly ex-tour-company minivans and larger trucks complete with a locally-made body. What they all have in common is that they're grossly overloaded (16 passengers in a 9-seat minivan) and are driven at breakneck speed. The origin of the meaning of the word 'Matatu' appears to be that it used to cost 30 cents (three 10-cent coins) to travel in Nairobi: *tatu* is the Swahili word for three .

Health Services

In 1991 (the most up-to-date figures available) Kenya had 277 hospitals, 357 health centres and 1712 dispensaries, as well as a number of mission hospitals and clinics in the country's more remote areas. There is, in Kenya, one doctor for every 6850 people, one dentist for every 38,600, and one nurse for every 900 people. Leading hospitals are the Nairobi Hospital, Aga Khan, Gertrude's Garden Children's Hospital, M.P. Shah and the Mater Misericordia.

Education

At Independence, Kenya had 5000 primary and 222 secondary schools, 8 technical institutes, 35 teachers' colleges and 1 technical college. By 1991, these figures had risen to 15,196 primary and 2647 secondary schools, 38 technical institutes, 22 teachers' training colleges and four universities.

Below: *Kenya's major centres are connected by regular and inexpensive buses known as matatus.*

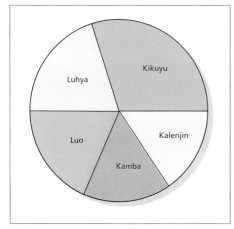

Kikuyu

Luhya

Luo

Kalenjin

Kamba

MAJOR ETHNIC GROUPS

THE PEOPLE

Man's earliest ancestors may well have originated as long as five million years ago in what is now northern Kenya. One wouldn't be far wrong in saying that the country's indigenous population represents more diversity than any other African country; approximately 30 languages are spoken in Kenya.

The most populous ethnic group is the Kikuyu, which numbered 3,202,800 at the last census; the smallest group is the el-Molo, living on the shores of Lake Turkana; they are probably less than 500 strong. Kenya's population has increased two and a half times since Independence and in 1993 was estimated to have reached at least 24.4 million.

Although the urban population continues to increase as people move to the cities and towns in search of jobs, better education opportunities and health facilities, at least 80% of Kenya's population lives in the rural areas. Life expectancy now stands at 60 years; more than half the population is below the age of 14, and this inevitably puts a heavy burden on education and health facilities.

Below: *sisal plantations in the Mogotio area. Other important national crops include tea, coffee, pineapples and pyrethrum.*

Culture

The majority of Kenyans are ambivalent toward their culture; they would prefer to have the world perceive them as a part of modern and progressive society than as stereotyped tribal warriors.

Religion

Along the country's coast and in its eastern provinces, most Kenyans are followers of Islam. **Islamic** sects make up 30% of Kenya's population, the remainder are **Christians** of various denominations. Almost every Christian sect is represented, as well as a number of **African Christian** groups which owe no allegiance to any of the world's Christian denominations. There has been an upsurge in these indigenous sects, and they are viewed with some suspicion by the government, who consider many of these sects to be radical.

COMMON SWAHILI WORDS	
English	**Swahili**
Hello	Jambo
How are you?	Habari?
I'm fine/good/well	Mzuri
Thank you	Asante
Please/excuse me	Tafadhali
Yes	Ndiyo
No	Hapana
Today	Leo
Tomorrow	Kesho
Hot	Moto
Cold	Baridi
Hotel	Hoteli
Room	Chumba
Bed	Kitanda
Shop	Duka

Most followers of Islam are of the Sunni branch, who have been able to attract reliable funding from Saudi Arabia for schools and hospitals. Among the Asian people, the most influential is the Ismaili community, followers of the Aga Khan. The Aga Khan has been liberal with funding in Kenya; as a result, many hospitals and schools are named after him. There is also a large following of **Hindus** of various sects.

Language

Kenya's official language is **English**, with **Swahili** the lingua franca readily understood by the majority of the people. In addition, all will speak their tribal mother tongue, such as Ki-Kikuyu and Ki-Maasai.

Left: *a Muslim fruit merchant displays his wares on a Mombasa sidewalk. All the major faiths are represented in Kenya: nearly 2000 religious organizations are registered within the country. Most of the people are Christians; Islam has the largest minority following.*

GOLF COURSES GALORE

Kenya has a number of beautifully scenic golf courses at various altitudes, from sea level right up to the nine-hole Molo Hills Hotel golf course, at 2740m (8989ft). The newest is that at the Windsor Golf and Country Club; the oldest is the Royal Nairobi; its 'Royal' title was bestowed on the then Nairobi Golf Club in 1935 by King George V. The Muthaiga and Karen golf clubs each have championship courses. Kisumu Golf Club, on the shores of Lake Victoria, has a very interesting rule which could only apply in Africa: 'If the ball comes to rest in dangerous proximity to a hippopotamus or a crocodile, another ball may be dropped at a safe distance, but no nearer the hole, without penalty.'

Sport and Recreation

To many people around the world, the words 'sport' and 'Kenya' mean one thing: athletics. Kenya's world-class middle- and long-distance runners have long dominated the running tracks of the world. The legendary Kipchoge 'Kip' Keino and Naftali Temu were the first in a long line of Kenya's runners to make a name for themselves worldwide in important international events (including the Olympic Games). Kenya has also done particularly well at boxing on an international level. But for most Kenyans, football (soccer) is the number-one sport. Kenya's national soccer team, the **Harambee Stars**, has won the East and Central African Championships eight times since 1967, and in 1987 it was runner-up to Egypt in the fourth All Africa Games. Kenya's football clubs have upheld a very good record in international tournaments, winning nine East and Central African Club Championships since 1974. The most successful football clubs are Gor Mahia (who in 1987 won the Nelson Mandela Cup in the African Cup Winners), AFC Leopards and Kenya Breweries.

Other popular sports in Kenya are hockey, cricket, golf, tennis, rugby and squash. Both freshwater and deep-sea fishing, and polo attract the sports enthusiast and, of course, so does the world-famous Safari Rally held every Easter, when the world's leading rally drivers battle it out over 4500km (2795 miles) of rugged road and track.

Kenya offers an endless selection of sports opportunities for both the active player and the spectator. There are over 40 different sporting associations and management bodies in Kenya to look after a wide variety of activities and events.

Food

Most visitors to Kenya are surprised by the quality of food served at safari lodges and camps: in the mobile safari camps, cooks (*mpishis*) prepare it in old ammunition boxes covered in hot ashes. Breakfast and lunch are usually enjoyed in the shade of a tree, adding to the occasion. Breakfast consists of fresh paw-paw, pineapple, melon and delicious finger-sized bananas as well as fruit juices and porridge. English traditional bacon and eggs is also available. Often the cook is on hand to cook omelettes exactly to order. Lunch offers a selection of cold meats, fish and salads as well as a hot meal. Indian curry for Sunday lunch has become traditional. Saturday lunch often features African dishes such as *irio* (mashed peas, potatoes and maize), *nyama choma* (roast meat), *ugali* (stiff maize porridge), *sukuma wiki* (cooked spinach mixed with tomato and onion), *kuku* (chicken), *matoke* (steamed bananas) and *githeri* (mashed beans and maize). International cuisine is usually served at dinner.

Visitors staying at the coast will sample Kenya's wonderful seafood: oysters, lobsters, crab and a host of sea fish. Nairobi offers the visitor a bewildering choice of restaurants of different nationalities. True Swahili cuisine is best found at the coast.

DRINKS ARE SERVED

World renowned, Kenya's beers are Tusker, Whitecap, Pilsner, Tusker Premium and Tusker Export. The first three come in 500ml bottles, while Tusker Premium and Tusker Export are in 300ml bottles. Wine drinkers are well catered for as wines imported from all over the world are available. Kenya now has its own vineyards on the shores of Lake Naivasha, which are producing credible wines. After-dinner liqueurs – 'Kenya Gold', a coffee liqueur, and 'Ivory Cream', a coffee-cream liqueur – complete the mouthwatering delights on offer in Kenya.

2
Central Kenya

Kenya's central highlands are dominated by the imposing peaks of **Mount Kenya** and the fertile, forested slopes of the **Aberdare** mountain range. A region of high plateaus, rolling green foothills and moorlands, its most distinctive feature is a rich diversity of giant alpine flora in the mountainous upper reaches. Among the plant species are thickets of bamboo, gnarled hagenia trees, giant heather, tussock grass and groundsels (senecio), some of which grow to over 10m (33ft).

The **Aberdare National Park** itself lies mostly above 3048m (10,000ft); because the Aberdares form a barrier to the prevailing easterly winds, the rainfall on the upper slopes is as high as 2000mm (80in), making this a major water catchment area. The region's well-watered foothills support undulating plantations of coffee and tea. Two major rivers cross the area, the east-flowing Athi, and the Tana which is fed by streams running off the slopes of Mount Kenya and which supplies the country with its main source of hydroelectric power.

Nairobi, the United Nations regional headquarters, forms the area's hub and is important internationally as both a commercial and a communication centre. It offers visitors many worthwhile sights, and there is lots to do. Of the city's many mosques and temples, don't miss seeing the interesting – and photogenic – **Jamia Mosque**. And even though most tourists passing through the city are safari-goers, **Nairobi National Park** with its varied wildlife grazing against the backdrop of the city skyline should be included in one's intinerary.

CLIMATE

Although it is situated only 33km (21 miles) south of the equator, Nairobi lies at an altitude of 1675m (5496ft) and therefore enjoys a **pleasant year-round** climate with cool evenings and mornings, and an average daytime temperature of 24–29°C (75–85°F). From June to August it is often **cloudy, overcast** and **cool** but the other months, even in the rainy seasons, are usually **bright and sunny**.

Opposite: *Nairobi's attractive skyline.*

DON'T MISS

*** Nairobi National Park, five minutes out of the city
*** National Museum for pre-historic displays on origins of man; natural history exhibits
*** Aberdare National Park; prolific wildlife in thick forest habitat
** Railway Museum; traces the history of the 'lunatic line'
** Karen Blixen Museum; beautifully preserved home
** A night's game-viewing at Treetops or The Ark.

NAIROBI

Driving from the airport into Nairobi, one of the most prominent buildings on the skyline is the **Kenyatta Conference Centre** (its main hall can seat 4000 delegates); a public viewing platform on the 28th floor affords sweeping vistas across the city. The birth of Nairobi occurred less than 100 years ago, on 30 May 1899, when the chief engineer of Uganda Railway Construction, George Whitehouse, chose the spot for the railhead ('Mile 327') roughly halfway between Mombasa and Kampala, before tackling the difficult Rift Valley Escarpment. Prior to this, apart from the Maasai who watered their cattle in the river, the first European to live in the area was Sergeant Ellis of the Royal Engineers, who operated a telegraph office there. With the arrival of the railway, Nairobi quickly grew and by 1907 had become the capital of British East Africa.

Nairobi is now the largest city in east and central Africa, with a population of over two million. Often referred to as the 'city in the sun' or 'city of flowers,' the mostly broad streets and open areas, dominated by modern high-rise buildings, are lined with bougainvillea, jacaranda and hibiscus. The quiet suburbs of **Muthaiga**, **Limuru**, **Karen** and **Langata** have large homes set in beautiful spacious gardens, all of which contrast with the shanty towns which exist in and alongside the city.

National Museum ***

The National Museum is a must for every visitor to Nairobi. Originally known as the Coryndon Museum after Sir Robert Coryndon who was the main benefactor in its early days, it is perhaps best known for its connection with Dr Louis Leakey, the famous palaeontologist. The museum is well laid out, with cultural and historic sections, and good displays on birds, insects, reptiles, fish and mammals. The work of Joy Adamson is well represented with exhibits of her tribal portraits, and her Kenya flower and plant watercolours.

In the grounds of the museum is a **snake park** and an **aquarium**, both very popular with visitors. Some of the snakes are in open pits, while others are behind glass.

The National Museum is open daily from 09:30 to 18:00; from Monday to Friday there are voluntary guides who speak a number of languages to help visitors find their way around.

Above: *the Delamere Terrace of the Norfolk Hotel in Nairobi.*

Railway Museum **

The museum is close to Uhuru Highway, but is best approached from the railway station. Among the old locomotives on display outside the museum buildings is the carriage Charles Ryall was dragged out of by a maneating lion in Tsavo National Park. Ryall, a young police superintendent who volunteered to shoot the lions taking their toll of railway workers, fell asleep and became a victim himself. The museum houses a very interesting collection of memorabilia tracing the railway's history, including wonderful old photographs.

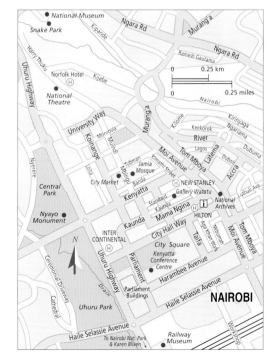

Nairobi National Park ★★★

Kenya's first national park at the time and only 8km
(5 miles) from the city centre, Nairobi National Park was
opened in 1946. This unique area, entirely within the city
limits, is only 120km^2 (44 sq miles) and is home to an
amazing variety of wildlife: 80 mammal and over 500
bird species have been recorded.

Fenced on three sides, the fourth boundary is formed
by the Athi River, affording access to migrating game.
Unfortunately Kitengela, once a traditional Maasai grazing area across the river, is slowly being settled which
will hinder any future migration.

Most of the park is made up of open plains and scattered acacia bush, with a handful of man-made dams
holding permanent water and intersected by a number of
small seasonal rivers; in the west, an extensive area of
highland forest contains olive and Cape chestnut trees.

Nairobi National Park is perhaps the best place to see
the endangered black rhino, which occurs in good numbers (approximately 40 individuals) and is quite tame. It
is also a good place to see and photograph Africa's
largest antelope, the eland, which unusually is not at all
shy or skittish here. Masai giraffe, buffalo, warthog and

Below: *the Nairobi
National Park.*

both Thomson's and Grant's gazelle are all common. Predators are well represented: lion and cheetah are quite a common sight, leopard are occasionally spotted in the highland forest. Strangely, hyena are seldom encountered, but it is not unusual to spot silver-backed jackal. During the dry season, there is a large influx of game – mainly wildebeest, kongoni (Coke's hartebeest) and zebra – from the Athi-Kapiti Plains.

Nairobi Animal Orphanage ⋆

Located just inside the national park's main entrance gate, the orphanage was founded in 1963 to look after, and later return to the wilderness, sick and abandoned wild animals. Although this is still the main aim of the orphanage, a number of the animals are now permanent residents – among these a pair of tigers – so in many ways it is really very much a zoo. Any abandoned young elephants and rhinos are cared for nearby by author and conservationist Daphne Sheldrick. Her experiences while rearing a variety of African wildlife, particularly elephants, are told in her books *The Tsavo Story* and *An Elephant Called Eleanor*. Visitors wishing to view any animals in residence should call Daphne at tel: (02) 891996 for an appointment. Nearby is the **Wildlife Education Centre** which shows wildlife films to children on weekend afternoons and holidays.

CAPE CHESTNUT

The Cape chestnut (*Calodendrum capense*) is one of the most beautiful flowering trees in the highlands of Kenya. It grows up to 20m (66ft) high and during the summer when it flowers, the forests are filled with beautiful rosy-pink blossoms. The trees are particularly common along the Rift Valley Escarpment near Nairobi.

Above: *residents of Nairobi National Park graze within a stone's throw of the city. Tallest of the buildings is the Kenyatta Conference Centre, whose 28th floor has an observation platform.*

Giraffe Manor **

Giraffe Manor, 18km (11 miles) from Nairobi, along the route to the Blixen Museum, was the home of Jock and Betty Leslie Melville, who in 1976 turned their home into the **Langata Nature Education Centre** and founded the African Fund for Endangered Wildlife (AFEW). The purpose of the centre was to help preserve the Rothschild's giraffe which was threatened at the time, and also to educate young Kenyans about conservation. Originally two Rothschild's giraffe – Daisy and Marlon – were transported to the centre from western Kenya, where the human population was spreading increasingly into their territory. A circular wooden building housing a small lecture theatre has been constructed, around which is a raised platform from where visitors can feed and observe the giraffe; this has proved very popular with children. One can stay overnight at Giraffe Manor.

Worth visiting nearby is **Utamaduni**, a large house which contains a number of rooms selling various Kenyan crafts. It also has a very good coffee shop.

Set in peaceful scenic grounds is **Ostrich Park**, an arts and crafts village near Utamaduni. Ostriches reared here are a big attraction, as are the wood carvers, and carpet and basket weavers, all of whom can be watched at work.

WHAT TO BUY

- Kiondos (traditional hand-woven sisal baskets)
- African-print batiks, leather belts, necklaces
- Wooden or soapstone carvings
- Semiprecious stones: tsavorite (a type of green garnet), tanzanite (sapphire-blue stone from Tanzania), jade and malachite
- Africana books (available in Nairobi at much cheaper prices than in Europe or the USA).

Above: *the one-time home of Karen Blixen has been carefully restored and now serves as a museum.*
Opposite: *walking through emerald tea plantations in Kenya's high, rolling Limuru uplands.*

Karen Blixen Museum **

This museum, once the home of Baroness Karen von Blixen, is located in the Nairobi suburb of Karen, which was named after her. Also famous as Isak Dinesen, the author of *Letters From Africa, Shadows on the Grass* and *Out of Africa* (this was turned into a major motion picture starring Meryl Streep), Karen Blixen lived here from 1914 to 1931. The house has been beautifully restored to its former state. Most of the furnishings are original but a few items, including the cuckoo clock and the bookcase (belonging to Dennis Finch Hatton) are replicas, made specially for the film *Out of Africa*. The house, open daily, is set in a large, colourful garden which was part of the old coffee farm. The view behind the homestead is dominated by the Ngong Hills, loved so much by Karen; the name 'Ngong' is a mispronunciation of the Maasai name for the hills, 'Enkongu e Mpakasi', meaning 'source of the Embakasi River'. Nearby is a small restaurant called the Karen Blixen Coffee Garden, once part of the coffee estate and home to the estate manager. It still retains its atmosphere from the past and the food is excellent. There is also a small gift shop.

Limuru Uplands

Limuru, 30km (18 miles) north of Nairobi, is at a bracing altitude of 2225m (7300ft) and set among rolling green hills covered with tea and coffee plantations. Tea, the main crop in the area, was first planted near here in 1903;

in 1910 a Mr Mitchell was responsible for the planting of the first commercial tea estate. Picking takes place most mornings, and only the new, young, tender shoots are plucked, giving the bushes their characteristic flat-topped shape. One can visit a tea estate by prior arrangement; Mr Mitchell's daughter organizes tours and lunches at her **Kiambethu Tea Estate**.

Limuru town is the home of Bata Shoe Company, which produces nine million pairs of shoes a year.

Thika

Forty-five kilometres (28 miles) north of Nairobi is the town of **Thika**, made famous by author Elspeth Huxley's *Flame Trees of*

> **BOMAS OF KENYA**
>
> The Bomas is a cultural centre set in 33ha (82 acres) of ground near Langata, 10km (6 miles) from Nairobi. The centre is dominated by a large circular building which can hold 3500 people; here visitors can watch a display of professional dancers representing various Kenyan ethnic groups. Outside is a display of various different tribal homes illustrating different construction methods. In the main building, a restaurant serves ethnic foods. The Bomas are open daily, performances take place every afternoon.

COLOBUS MONKEY

These magnificent black-and-white monkeys are common in both the Aberdare and Mount Kenya national parks. They can usually be observed in the forest, leaping spectacularly – arms and legs outstretched – from tree to tree in search of food. Colobus monkeys differ from others in that they have no thumb; they feed almost exclusively on tender young leaves, spending the rest of the day grooming each other or resting. Young monkeys are born completely white, remaining that way for about a month, after which they slowly turn black and white. The colobus is a protected species.

Thika. The Blue Posts Inn, featured in the book, is still in operation and is worth a visit. In the hotel grounds are the **Chania Falls** which were used as the location for a Tarzan movie some years ago. Nowadays Thika is best known for its Del Monte pineapple plantations, the largest in the world (Kenya is the world's third largest pineapple producer). The town also has a vehicle assembly plant handling British Land-Rovers among others.

Twenty kilometres (12 miles) away on the Thika to Garissa road are the popular **Fourteen Falls**. Although they are not high (only 27m; 89ft), they can be quite spectacular, especially after the rains. Surrounded by dense tropical vegetation, the falls are a popular picnic spot at weekends.

Ol Doinyo Sabuk National Park ✶

Near to the Fourteen Falls is the entrance to Ol Doinyo Sabuk National Park, itself a large forest-covered hill

2146m (7040ft) high. Ol Doinyo Sabuk, meaning 'sleeping buffalo' in Maasai, has only one track suitable for motor vehicles, winding its way to the summit through dense highland forest. The view on a clear day is wonderful – Mount Kenya and Nairobi can both be clearly seen. About halfway along this rough track is a panoramic bluff which offers wonderful views over the countryside. Here are three marble plaques, set on slabs of rock; they are the graves of Sir William Northrup Macmillan, his wife and their servant Louise Decker. Sir William, a wealthy American who loved the spot, was one of the early settlers in the area and owned the nearby 8049ha (19,890 acres) Juja Ranch. Although the park has a good population of game including buffalo, bushbuck, leopard

Left: *the renowned Treetops Lodge in the Aberdare park.*
Opposite: *the lovely Chania Falls at Thika, about which author Elspeth Huxley wrote so movingly. The area is notable for its vast pineapple plantations.*

and colobus monkeys, it is often very difficult to spot them because of the thick forest. There are many interesting birds, among them Hartlaub's turaco, white-starred forest robin and Narina trogon. It is advisable not to leave your vehicle unattended or to visit the area alone.

ABERDARE NATIONAL PARK

The Aberdare National Park, 100km (62 miles) north of Nairobi, covers an area of 767km² (296 sq miles). Now officially called **Nyandarua** (a Kikuyu name meaning 'a drying hide'), the Aberdares were given their original name by the explorer Thomson, who first saw the mountains in 1884 and named them after Lord Aberdare, then president of the Royal Geographical Society.

The park consists of the Aberdare mountain range running north to south, and a thickly forested salient which extends down the eastern slopes. On the eastern and western sides, montane forest slowly gives way to bamboo and hagenia at the higher levels. In the north is **Ol Doinyo Satima**, the highest peak at 3995m (13,100ft), and in the south the **Kinangop**. Between the two is an undulating moorland at an altitude of 3000m (9840ft), with scattered rocky outcrops, forest patches, highland bogs and streams. The moorland is covered in tussock grass, with areas of giant heaths, groundsels (senecios) and forest patches of rosewood, St John's wort and bamboo. A number of ice-cold streams cross the moorland,

---

BEAUTIFUL WATERFALLS

● Of the waterfalls in Aberdare National Park, the most accessible and widely photographed are the Chania Falls – sometimes known as Queen's Cave Waterfall after a visit by Queen Elizabeth II, who had lunch in a wooden pavilion overlooking the cascade.

● The Gura Falls, Kenya's highest at 457m (1500ft), are the most spectacular but unfortunately it is only possible to stand at the top of them, so their true magnitude cannot be seen.

● The Karura Falls, situated opposite the Gura, drop down to merge at the confluence of the two rivers a little further on.

LORD BADEN-POWELL

Lord Baden-Powell, founder of the Boy Scouts movement, first visited Kenya in 1935. While staying in the small town of Nyeri, he is quoted as saying, 'The nearer to Nyeri, the nearer to bliss.' In 1938 he retired, returning to Nyeri to live in a cottage named Paxtu, specially built for him in the Outspan Hotel grounds. He and his wife, Lady Olave, lived here until his death on 8 January 1941. They are both buried facing Mount Kenya, in the nearby churchyard of St Peter's Church. Inscribed on Lord Baden-Powell's tombstone is a circle and dot, the Boy Scout symbol for 'gone home'. With permission from the Outspan Hotel one can visit Paxtu, which remains much as it was in the Baden-Powells' time.

eventually cascading down the slopes in a series of waterfalls. These streams hold both brown and rainbow trout, and there are two fishing camps on the moorland to cater for keen anglers.

The heavy rainfall in this catchment area makes the tracks very difficult to navigate and four-wheel-drive vehicles are essential. Animal life is prolific, but the thick forest habitat impedes game-viewing. Elephant, rhino, buffalo, giant forest hog, bushbuck and both colobus and Syke's monkeys are all common. Predators are well represented, among them lion, leopard, hyena and serval (many of them melanistic). Birdlife too is abundant and varied: cinnamon-chested bee-eaters nest in holes alongside the park's tracks, the crowned eagle – Africa's most powerful – is common in the forest where it preys on suni (a tiny antelope, smaller than a dik-dik), while mountain buzzards circle over the moorlands and Jackson's francolins, only found in Kenya, forage for food in the coarse tussock grass.

The most convenient way to visit and experience the Aberdares is to spend a night at **The Ark** or **Treetops**, night game-viewing lodges located in the Salient (*see* p. 41). The whole of this wonderful area is surrounded by small African farms (*shambas*) and large coffee estates. Because of the conflict between wildlife and farmer, the

whole of the national park is in the process of being surrounded by an electric fence, powered by water-driven generators.

The enormous cost of this project is mostly being supported by local donations; an organization called Rhino Ark arranges fund-raising events such as motosport and golf.

Mount Kenya is becoming increasingly popular with mountaineers from all over the world (Reinhold Messner, the first man to climb Mount Everest without oxygen, did much of his high-altitude and ice training on Mount Kenya). The main central peaks, Batian and Nelion, require ropes and ice axes, and a certain degree of proficiency; Lenana is suitable for climbers with little experience. The four main routes to the peaks are: Naro Moru, the Sirimon and Timau tracks on the mountain's western slopes, and the Chogoria route on the eastern slopes. One can take a circular route or use a different track on the return leg (only for the experienced climber). Vegetation varies from dense forest and bamboo jungle to gnarled hagenia trees draped with 'old man's beard'. Contact the Naro Moru River Lodge for details.

MOUNT KENYA NATIONAL PARK

Mount Kenya, at 5199m (17,058ft) the country's highest mountain, has its higher slopes permanently covered in snow and ice, even though it sits astride the equator. The national park comprises the mountain above the 3200m (10,500ft) contour plus two salients astride the Naro Moru and Sirimon routes. Called 'Kirinyaga' by the Kikuyu to whom it is sacred, the first European to climb Mount Kenya was Sir Halford Mackinder, in 1899. An old extinct volcano, it is made up of three peaks: **Batian** (the highest), **Nelion** and **Lenana**. Of these peaks, the original hard centre core is all that remains; the bulk of the volcano has been eroded away with time.

Although conceived as a recreation area, the park has a good and varied population of wildlife, and is of geological and botanical interest. Elephant, buffalo and rhino are frequently seen as one slowly climbs upwards, and even when one is in the alpine zone just below the main peaks, there is wildlife in the form of giant rock hyraxes, begging for food if given the chance! Birdlife too is varied. Walking through the forests you are sure to see a flash of vivid red as a Hartlaub's turaco flies ahead; you will no doubt hear the high-pitched squawks of flocks of red-headed parrots, and be startled by the raucous call and rushing sound of a silvery-cheeked hornbill's wings. The forest-covered mountain slopes below the park's boundary, containing many large

Above left: *Mount Kenya, viewed from the Aberdare National Park.*
Opposite: *the blossoms of Kenya's famed flame trees lend brilliant colour to city and countryside. Though three species – flamboyant, Australian and Nandi – thrive here, all are exotic.*

Podocarpus and lichen-covered olive trees, merge, as the altitude increases, into a zone of bamboo, some as high as 15m (49ft). This in turn blends into vegetation comprising mostly giant heath that often grows to tree size at this altitude. The area then becomes moorland covered in spiky tussock grass with giant lobelia and groundsels, some of which grow to a height of 4.5m (15ft). Growing among the tussock grass are patches of everlasting flowers, gladioli, delphiniums and red-hot pokers.

To the west of Mount Kenya is the **Laikipia Plateau**, mostly dry country of rolling plains dotted with acacia trees. This is cattle-ranching territory with a number of large ranch properties still inhabited by a variety of wildlife. In 1991 the 165km² (64 sq miles) **Laikipia National Reserve** was set up in the area. Several of the cattle ranches such as Colcheccio, Solio (which has been very successful in breeding both black and white rhino), El Karama and Segera are now open to visitors and provide a different type of safari that offers horse riding, walking and fishing.

Night Game-viewing Lodges

Kenya has three night game-viewing lodges where powerful spotlights are directed onto a nearby waterhole and salt lick. Two of these tree hotels, **Treetops** and **The Ark**, are situated in the salient of the Aberdare National Park, while the third, **Mountain Lodge**, is on the slopes of Mount Kenya. Visitors to Treetops are first taken to Outspan Hotel in Nyeri for lunch; afterwards, guests are entertained by Kikuyu drummers in traditional dress. Visitors to The Ark lunch at the Aberdares Country Club.

MT KENYA SAFARI LODGES

Around the base of the mountain are a number of hotels and lodges:
- The plush Mount Kenya Safari Club, for guests who demand the utmost in comfort and luxury
- Mountain Lodge, a night game-viewing lodge similar to The Ark and Treetops
- The Naro Moru River Lodge, simple but beautifully situated, specializes in assisting mountaineers to climb the mountain safely; good for bird-watching
- The KenTrout Grill and Cottages for a delicious trout meal or for an overnight stay in rustic but comfortable surroundings; excellent value.

Top: *the Mount Kenya Safari Club.*
Opposite: *The Ark, a lodge that has a viewing walkway among the tree tops.*

At both venues, guests are transported to their respective night-viewing lodges. Mountain Lodge is similar, but differs in that you drive directly to the lodge where all meals will be are taken, giving you more time to enjoy the highland forest scene; it is also not such a rush to leave in the morning.

Because The Ark is deep inside the salient, the drive there often reveals colobus and Syke's monkeys, buffalo and elephant. At each tree hotel, tea and cakes are served; often there is already game at the waterhole. Each hotel has a photographic bunker and/or open verandah where visitors can watch and photograph the wildlife. Flash photography is not allowed.

The Ark has a walkway among the tree tops, good for bird-watchers. A bird-feeding table attracts large numbers of birds, while underneath, waiting for scraps, is usually a black-tipped mongoose and occasionally a pair of suni. As the daylight fades, powerful spotlights are switched on. Dinner is served at eight, but guests keep their binoculars at hand as an interesting animal might appear at any time. It is important to be as quiet as possible. One need not worry about missing anything when retiring to bed, as a bell in each room will ring the minute an interesting animal is sighted. A warm fire burns all night (the lodges are at a height of around 2133m (6998ft) so nights can be very chilly); tea and coffee is also served the night through. Early the next morning, guests are transported back to the Outspan or Aberdares Country Club, where they meet up again with their safari guide and vehicle.

Central Kenya at a Glance

BEST TIMES TO VISIT

The best time is from **December to mid-March** when days are hot, sunny and dry, and nights are usually cool. Also nicest time to climb Mount Kenya, as peaks are normally cloud free. The main rainy season occurs mid-March to May, with a shorter period of rain in November.

GETTING THERE

Main Nairobi–Nakuru and Nairobi–Nanyuki **roads** are **tarred** and generally good. Condition of roads poor except for some of major toll roads running through Nairobi and Mombasa. For security, try not to travel after dark.

GETTING AROUND

There are three types of **taxi** in Nairobi: the best but most expensive is a Mercedes from Kenatco Taxis; next, the black London-type cab; finally, taxis with a thick yellow line along the side (old but cheap). Kenatco Taxis charge a set price per km, tel: (02) 225123 or 221561. It is customary to bargain with the others, but make sure you agree on the price before getting in.

To get to the national parks, most visitors join an **organized tour**. It is possible, though, to **hire a car** in Nairobi and visit the parks on your own (major car-hire firms are represented). Try Avis, tel: (02) 36794 or 34317, or Hertz UTC, tel: (02) 31960.

WHERE TO EAT

If one joins a safari to any of the national parks and reserves, all meals are catered for by the lodges at which guests are staying. Visitors staying in self-help bandas can usually buy a midday meal at a safari lodge.

Nairobi
Alan Bobbe's Bistro, Koinange St: the best of French cuisine, tel: (02) 226027/4945.
Foresta Magnetica, Corner House, Kimathi and Mama Ngina sts: Italian cooking, tel: (02) 728009 or 223662.
Tamarind Restaurant, Harambee Ave: renowned for its seafood, tel: (02) 338959.
Minar Restaurant, Banda St: Indian fare, tel: (02) 330168 or 227612.
Marino's, Aga Khan Walk: Italian cuisine, tel: (02) 336210/7230.
La Galleria, Casino, Museum Hill: Italian food, tel: (02) 742600 or 744477.
Safeer, Tom Mboya St: spicy Indian, tel: (02) 336803.
Carnivore, Langata Rd: famous for its game dishes, tel: (02) 501775.

Hotel Restaurants
Ibis Grill and **The Lord Delamere**, Norfolk Hotel: nouvelle cuisine at the former, international menu at the latter, tel: (02) 335422.
Mandhari, and **Cafe Maghreb,** both located in the Nairobi Serena Hotel: international cuisine, high standard, tel: (02) 710511.
The Tate Room, New Stanley Hotel: offers fine cuisine, tel: (02) 333248.
Le Bougainville, Safari Park Hotel: international menu, tel: (02) 802493; Korean, Japanese, French and African cuisine also served.
Windsor Room, Windsor Golf and Country Club: French-influenced menu, tel: (02) 219784.

WHERE TO STAY

Nairobi
Norfolk Hotel, Harry Thuku Rd: the rich and famous have stayed here; Nairobi's meeting place, tel: (02) 335422, fax: 336742.
Nairobi Serena Hotel, Central Park, Kenyatta Ave: set in beautiful gardens, its restaurants recommended, tel: (02) 725111, fax: 725184.
Safari Park Hotel, Thika Rd: large and lavish, set in 64 acres of land, tel: (02) 802493, fax: 802477.
Nairobi Safari Club, University Way: distinctive high-rise fountain in foyer, tel: (02) 330621, fax: 331201.
Windsor Golf and Country Club, Garden Estate: elegant, looks onto beautiful golf course, tel: (02) 217444, fax: 802322.
New Stanley Hotel, Kimathi St: has acacia rising in middle of its cafe to which hunters and travellers used to pin messages, tel: (02) 333233, fax: 229388.

Central Kenya at a Glance

Nairobi Hilton, Mama Ngina St: tall, circular, tower-like hotel with rooftop pool, tel: (02) 334000, fax: 339463.
Giraffe Manor, outside Nairobi: tel: (02) 891078.

Limuru Uplands
Kentmere Club, near Tigoni country inn atmosphere, set in lovely gardens, tel: (0154) 41053 or 42101.

Aberdares
Aberdare Country Club, Nyeri: elegant country home set in landscaped gardens, book through Lonrho Hotels.
Outspan Hotel, Nyeri: site of Baden-Powell's home, still used as a suite for guests, book through Block Hotels.

Mount Kenya
Mount Kenya Safari Club, nine-hole golf course; bird observation towers, pools, book through Lonrho Hotels.
Sweetwaters Tented Camp, on Ol Pejeta Ranch: solitude in luxury thatched tents set in rhino sanctuary, book through Lonrho Hotels.
Naro Moru River Lodge, Naro Moru: set in Mt Kenya foothills, book through Alliance Hotels.
Ken Trout Grill & Cottages: guest houses on peaceful farm, call telephone operator (900) and ask for Timau 14, or tel: (02) 228391.

Ranches
Colcheccio Lodge: write to Richard Bonham Safaris Ltd,

PO Box 24133, Nairobi; tel: (02) 882521, fax: 882728.
Sangare Ranch: book through Safcon Travel Services.
Segera Ranch: book through Bush Homes of East Africa.
Ol Ari Nyiro Ranch: contact the Gallman Memorial Foundation, PO Box 45593, Nairobi; fax: (02) 521220.
El Karama Ranch: self-catering *bandas*, book through Let's Go Travel.

Night Game-viewing Lodges
Aberdares
The Ark: tree hotel built in form of Noah's Ark, book through Lonrho Hotels.
Treetops: wooden hotel on stilts, visited by Queen Elizabeth and Prince Philip, book through Block Hotels.

Mount Kenya
Mountain Lodge: hotel on stilts in heart of rainforest; book through African Tours and Hotels.

Tours and Excursions
Camel safaris: Camel Trek Ltd, tel: (02) 891079, fax: 891716; Desert Rose Camels Ltd, tel: (02) 228936, fax: 212160; Just The Ticket, tel: (02) 74155/6/7.

Horseback safaris: Safaris Unlimited (Africa) Ltd, tel: (020) 891168/0435, fax: 891113; Offbeat Safaris Ltd, book through Bush Homes of East Africa.
Walking safaris: Kentreck Safaris Ltd, book through Let's Go Travel, tel: (02) 340331, fax: 336890; Alliance Hotels central booking office, tel: (02) 332825, fax: 219212; or contact Peter Faull, Samburu Trails Trekking Safaris, PO Box 40, Maralal.

Useful Addresses
African Tours and Hotels, Ltd, PO Box 30471, Nairobi; tel: (02) 336858, fax: 721618.
Alliance Hotels, PO Box 49839, Nairobi; tel: (02) 337501, fax: 219212.
Block Hotels Ltd, PO Box 47557, tel: (02) 335867, fax: 340541.
Bush Homes of East Africa Ltd, PO Box 56923, Nairobi; tel: (02) 506139, fax: 502739.
Lonrho Hotels Ltd, PO Box 58581, Nairobi; tel: (02) 216940, fax: 216796/6896.
Let's Go Travel, PO Box 60342, Nairobi; tel: (02) 340331, fax: 336890.
Safcon Travel Services Ltd, PO Box 59224, Nairobi; tel: (02) 503265, fax: 506824.

NAIROBI	J	F	M	A	M	J	J	A	S	O	N	D
AVERAGE TEMP. °F	68	68	70	70	66	64	63	63	68	66	66	66
AVERAGE TEMP. °C	20	20	21	21	19	18	17	17	20	19	19	19
Hours of Sun Daily	9	9	8	6	5	5	4	4	6	7	6	8
RAINFALL in	2	1	3	6	5	1	0	1	1	2	5	3
RAINFALL mm	50	37	85	154	125	30	14	19	20	49	132	77
Days of Rainfall	16	8	3	12	15	15	8	10	4	12	9	8

3
Western Kenya

Although this is the country's most highly populated region – and also the most productive with its vast rolling tea plantations and large wheat and maize-growing areas – Western Kenya is the least visited.

Only fairly recently has **Lake Victoria**, source of the Nile and the world's second largest freshwater lake, started arousing interest among visitors, because of the establishment of a number of exclusive new lodges there. Kenya's border with Uganda cuts through the lake's northeastern edge, and continues northwards to slice through the centre of **Mount Elgon**'s volcanic crater.

In contrast to the flatlands surrounding Lake Victoria's shores are the richly fertile slopes of the **Mau Escarpment** rising to the east, mantled with emerald tea plantations; rainfall on the Mau massif is abundant and regular. Sited in these highlands, the town of **Kericho** forms Kenya's tea capital.

The region's dense population is attributed to the Gusii people living in the highlands around **Kisii** (they are believed to support one of the highest birth rates in the world); the Luo, accomplished fishermen living around Lake Victoria's shores; and the Luhya of **Kakamega**, where the only remaining tropical rainforest in East Africa is to be seen.

Western Kenya's most famous area is, of course, the **Masai Mara National Reserve**, with its rolling grassland plains, acacia woodlands and scrub thickets which harbour a marvellously abundant variety of wildlife; and the open plains make game-viewing a pleasure.

Opposite: *game-viewing by balloon in the splendid Masai Mara National Reserve.*

MASAI MARA NATIONAL RESERVE

Kenya's premier wildlife area, the famous Masai Mara National Reserve, is a six-hour drive west of Nairobi. Lying at an altitude of 1650m (5414ft), it covers an area of 1510km² (580 sq miles) and forms the northern extension of the Serengeti National Park in Tanzania. The Mara, as it is generally known, is a Maasai word meaning 'spotted' or 'dappled'; it is a mosaic of rolling grassland dominated by red oat grass, small bush-covered hills, and along the Mara River and its tributaries flowing towards Lake Victoria, riverine bush and forest.

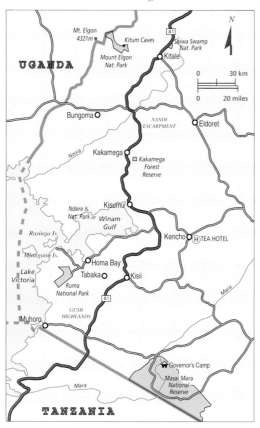

The reserve is well known for its black-maned lion, as well as its abundant resident wildlife, and is one of the few places where it's possible to see the 'big five' during a morning's game drive. However, it is perhaps more famous for its annual wildebeest migration – possibly Africa's greatest wildlife spectacle. The wildebeest population is now thought to number 1.4 million; accompanying them into the Mara may be as many as 550,000 gazelle, 200,000 zebra and 64,000 impala. Added to this are rhino, elephant, buffalo, warthog, giraffe, topi, kongoni (Coke's hartebeest), eland, leopard, cheetah, hyena and jackal – 95 species of mammal in all. Many of the cheetah are so tame they seek shelter from the hot sun under

UGANDA • Mount Elgon
            Nat. Park

            • Kisumu
Lake
Victoria   Homa Bay   • Kericho

            Ruma   • Kisii
            National Park

TANZANIA   Masai Mara
                        National Reserve

Left: *tame cheetah in the Masai Mara. The park, perhaps the country's finest wildlife area and haven for the 'big five', is especially noted for its black-maned lion as well as its great wildebeest migrations.*

one's vehicle and several even climb onto the roof to get a better view of any prospective prey. For the bird enthusiast, almost 500 species have been recorded: among these are 16 species of eagle plus many hawks and falcons, six species of vulture, eight of stork, four of bustard (including the kori bustard, the world's heaviest flying bird), and nine species of sunbird. With this combination of wildlife and wonderful scenery, all under a great African sky, it is easy to see why the Masai Mara has become so popular among visitors.

It's possible to visit Lake Victoria while staying at the Masai Mara Reserve. At dawn, a light aircraft takes tourists to spend a morning fishing or sightseeing on the lake, usually returning after lunch.

Balloon Safaris ★★★

A popular event and an experience of a lifetime for visitors to the Masai Mara (and to the Taita Hills Lodge in southern Kenya) is a balloon flight. Participants gather at dawn at the launch site where they can watch the giant balloons being slowly inflated by motor-driven fans. The burners are then lit and, with a roar, the balloons quickly take shape. It is time to climb into the basket; the pilot instructs everyone on ballooning rules, and the burners are put on full power. Slowly, almost imperceptibly, the balloon leaves the ground and you are looking at the rising sun and the African bush below. The pilot soon

---

UP, UP AND AWAY

The world's first scheduled passenger service by balloon was launched in 1976 from Keekorok Lodge by Alan Root, the famous wildlife film maker, and the late balloon pilot, Dudley Chignal. Now, at least six lodges offer hot-air balloon flights, most of which are followed by a glorious champagne breakfast, making Kenya the only country in the world to offer such a high number of passenger balloon flights. It is now also possible to spot wildlife from the air by microlight aircraft.

CEREMONIAL RITES

No Maasai ceremony takes place without a bull, an ox or a cow, as the animal's blood plays an important role: while the animal's head is tightly held, the jugular vein is cut using the tip of an arrow or by shooting the arrow directly into the vein (the arrow has a leather thong wrapped around it just behind its tip to prevent it penetrating too far). Once the blood has been collected in a gourd, the vein is simply pinched and plugged with a wad of dung and mud. The blood is usually mixed with milk, but is also drunk untainted by warriors, by women who have just given birth, or by a person who has undergone circumcision rites.

CIRCUMCISION AND MARRIAGE RITES

Maasai girls are circumcised at puberty. Although a ceremony is held, it is limited to family as girls are not separated into age groups; circumcision takes place in the mother's house. Like the boys, the Maasai girls dress in black robes smeared with oil, and around their heads they wear a band which has long links of metal beads hanging from it to cover the eyes. After circumcision the girls are allowed to marry, but because men may only enter into marriage once they become elders, the girls' husbands are normally much older than they are.

points out animals and birds which mostly ignore the balloon unless it passes immediately over them. On a recent flight from Governors Camp in the Masai Mara reserve, a rare Pel's fishing owl was spotted on a nest which also contained a large young owl; this is the first breeding record in Kenya of the bird.

After about an hour, the balloon lands in an open area; the retrieving party arrives and before long a low dining table is set up and a full breakfast cooked over the balloon burners. While the food is being prepared, the pilot opens a bottle of champagne, and with everyone's glass full, a toast to the successful flight is proposed. Eating a cordon bleu breakfast surrounded by Africa cannot be beaten. After breakfast, guests are taken on a game drive while travelling back to their lodges.

The Maasai People

The Maasai are pastoralists, herding cattle, sheep and goats; they also keep donkeys as beasts of burden. The majority of the Maasai still remain firmly attached to their traditional life. After children, the most important aspect of their lives is cattle, which they believe were given to them by their god *Enkai*; a Maasai of modest wealth will own at least 50. (He will, however, only be considered wealthy if he also has children.) The beasts are rarely slaughtered for meat (special ceremonial occasions aside); instead they provide the Maasai people with all their needs: milk and blood for nourishment, hides for bedding and for making sandals, and as payment in the case of a dowry or fine.

The Maasai live in an *enk'ang*, or kraal – often wrongly called a *manyatta*, which is a collection of huts housing Maasai warriors. Low, igloo-shaped huts are constructed by the women out of thin branches and grass, which they cover with a mixture of cow dung and mud. The *enk'ang* is surrounded by a strong thorn-bush fence, and each evening cattle, sheep and goats belonging to all the families are herded into this enclosure until morning. The huts are usually divided into two or three alcoves: one is used as a sleeping area for very young calves, lambs and kids; the others form the Maasai sleeping areas and a cooking area.

A cultural feature of Maasai life is the male's passage through four traditional phases, each one marked by an important ceremony. The first one, called the *alamal lengipaata*, is performed just before circumcision. Because the circumcision ceremony only takes place every 12 to 15 years, the age of the boys taking part in the rites varies considerably. At this time, the group picks one of its members as a leader, who then retains the title throughout the lives of that particular group. The first phase is followed by *emorata*, or circumcision, initiating the boys into warriorhood. During the ceremony, the boys may show no sign of pain; to do so would be a disgrace. After a period of healing, they become warriors and are known as *morans*. They then become junior elders through the ceremony of *eunoto*, after which they may marry. Finally, with the *olngesherr* ceremony, they become senior elders whose duties are to preside over Maasai affairs. Traditionally the Maasai have no chiefs or headmen; all decisions are made by the senior elders.

Above: *Maasai woman.*
Opposite: *migratory wilde-beest in the Masai Mara.*

PASSAGE TO MANHOOD

Once male circumcision has taken place, a period of healing follows during which the boys daub their faces white and wear black robes. They use a small bow to shoot birds, which are fashioned into a special headdress – one way in which to prove their manhood and skills. A headdress can have as many as 50 birds. These circumcised young men travel all over Maasailand, and at the end of this period, the warriors grow their hair long, cover their bodies with ochre and dress in their finery.

HOMA BAY

The town of Homa Bay is 150km (93 miles) from Kisumu; from here one can hire a boat to visit Mfangano, Rusinga and Takawiri islands. This is also a base from which to visit Ruma National Park, a half-hour away. Originally known as Lambwe Valley, the park was established as a reserve primarily to protect roan antelope (a few do occur in the Masai Mara). The reserve lies in a long, narrow, tsetse-fly-infested valley; its wildlife species include oribi (another uncommon antelope in Kenya), Rothschild's giraffe, Jackson's hartebeest, topi, buffalo and zebra. It also has an interesting variety of birds.

LAKE VICTORIA

Visitors to the Masai Mara would hardly believe that only a few hours' drive away lies Lake Victoria, and the most populated area of Kenya. The major town in the area is **Kisumu**, Kenya's third largest. Like Nairobi, it owes its existence to the Uganda Railway which reached there in 1901; at the time the town was called Port Florence, after the wife of the chief railway engineer.

Kisumu sits on the shores of the **Winam Gulf**, a part of Lake Victoria. The lake covers an area of 68,000km^2 (26,255 sq miles) and is on average only 78m (255ft) deep. Living around its shores are the Luo people, who are both cultivators and expert fishermen (they sometimes refer to themselves as *Jonam*, the 'lake people'). They have adopted and still use today the boat style that originated from the traditional lateen-sailed dhows used by Arab slave-traders during the early part of this century.

During the day, the Luo fish for Nile perch (*mbuta*) and tilapia. The former was introduced into the lake from Lake Albert in Uganda some years ago and unfortunately has caused a drop in the population of many of the lake's smaller indigenous species; some have disappeared completely. Although the perch is a much larger fish and provides a lot of meat, tilapia is much preferred for its taste. At night fishermen throw out nets for a small sardine-like fish known as *omena*. They paddle out onto the lake and place floats holding bright kerosene lights on the water. The light attracts the fish, which are then caught using nets; these *omena* are spread out on the ground during the day to dry in the sun. The sight of the rainbow-coloured nets heaped along the shore and thousands of fish and African kites wheeling above is a feature of all the Luo lakeside villages.

Until recently very few tourists visited Lake Victoria, but with the opening of three small tourist lodges, the lake is slowly being rediscovered. Most tourists tend to be fishermen who fly to the lake from the Masai Mara for a pleasant day's angling.

The most beautiful of the lodges, **Mfangano Island Camp**, which comprises six cool, thatched-roof cottages styled after local Luo houses, is situated in a shady spot on Mfangano; there are others on Rusinga and Takawiri.

In the north of the Winam Gulf, about 30km (19 miles) across the water from Kisumu, is the tiny **Ndere Island National Park**, a rarely visited spot. It was gazetted a national park to protect its natural vegetation and bird-life; besides its hippo and crocodile population, it also harbours a small herd of impala.

SOAPSTONE CAPITAL

Inland from Homa Bay, situated in the Gusii highlands, is the town of Kisii, best known for its soapstone. The highlands' Gusii people are considered to be among the most artistic of Kenya's ethnic groups, and have produced some skilled soapstone sculptors. They also have one of the highest population densities in Kenya (and, supposedly, one of the highest birth rates in the world). The soapstone quarries, which supply much of the world with their rose-tinted product, lie a few miles south of Kisii, near Tabaka village.

Opposite and left: *fishing canoes near Dunga, a Luo village at Lake Victoria, the country's most densely populated region. Giant Nile perch have depleted the lake's smaller and tastier species, but the catches are still excellent and the fishing industry thrives.*

Kericho, Tea Centre

High in the western highlands, 98km (61 miles) from Kisii, is the town of Kericho, centre of Kenya's tea industry. Tea was first grown near here from Ceylonese and Indian plants in the 1920s; Kenya is now the world's third largest tea producer. The best place to see the plantations and watch the leaves being picked is from Kericho's renowned **Tea Hotel**, perched in the centre of the estate and surrounded by manicured lawns. Behind this elegant complex, originally built by Brooke Bond, visitors can walk amid the shoulder-high tea bushes and photograph the pickers with their wicker baskets.

In another highland area 73km (45 miles) north of Kisumu is the town of **Kakamega**, centre of the Luhya people. Kakamega's past claim to fame is the gold rush it experienced in the 1930s, which unfortunately didn't last very long. Gold is still found here, but only in small amounts. Nowadays Kakamega is known for its nearby forest which is unique in Kenya. Relict of a tropical rainforest that once extended from West to East Africa, it is home to trees, plants, animals and birds found nowhere else in Kenya. Forty-five square kilometres (17 sq miles) of the forest have been declared a national reserve.

Above: *the view across the tea plantations around Kericho. In addition to the estates there are many smallholdings, established as part of a unique farming scheme launched in 1963. Kenya is the world's third largest producer of tea.*
Opposite: *inside one of Mount Elgon's tube caves; the droppings are those of elephants, who visit the caverns in quest of mineral salts.*

Mount Elgon

Driving north from Kakamega, the immense bulk of Mount Elgon, its base over 80km (50 miles) across, soon dominates the skyline. It is Kenya's second highest mountain; the tallest peak, at 4321m (14,177ft), is actually in Uganda (Kenya's border bisects Elgon), the second highest in Kenya at 4310m (14,140ft) high. Part of the mountain, which is actually an extinct caldera, is a national park – one of the most scenic and unspoilt in the country. Elgon's lower slopes are forest-covered, containing some of Kenya's finest *Podocarpus* sp. trees, which slowly give way to beautiful afro-alpine moorland with giant heaths and groundsel. The crater floor, at an altitude of 3500m (11,480ft) comprises a luxuriant groundsel forest and has a number of hot springs which form the source of the Suam River.

One of Elgon's special features is that hiking and trout fishing are permitted in the national park. Mount Elgon also has a number of lava tube caves, some several hundred feet deep. Three are accessible, these being Kitum, Chepnyali and Mackingeny. Although the latter cave is the most spectacular, Kitum is the best known as it formed the subject of a wildlife film. Because mountain vegetation lacks minerals which are essential to the health of all wildlife, local elephants have for hundreds of years visited Mount Elgon's caves, particularly Kitum, to gouge into them – sometimes for quite long distances – in their constant search for essential mineral salts.

Other mammals also requiring these minerals, such as buffalo, bushbuck and duiker, have followed the elephants' path into the caves.

AFRO-ALPINE VEGETATION

The height of the alpine heath zone differs from mountain to mountain depending on rainfall and the direction of prevailing winds. Fascinating are the belts of giant heaths hung with strands of old man's beard; giant lobelias, some 3m (10ft) high, give way to giant groundsels which can grow to 9m (30ft). These high-altitude plants are specially adapted to withstand frost at night; the senecios, for example, close up tightly, only opening when the warm sun strikes them.

In Kenya this secretive antelope is found only along the shores of Lake Victoria and in the Saiwa National Park. The sitatunga's coat is dark and shaggy; rams have slightly spiralled, white-tipped horns. Characteristic of this antelope is its large splayed hoofs which can spread widely and are well suited to its swampy habitat; it swims readily too. The sitatunga feeds on reeds and grass during the day; the hottest hours are spent lying on cool, trampled reed mats.

Below: *a water-adapted sitatunga makes its way through the Saiwa Swamp.*

SAIWA SWAMP NATIONAL PARK

Due east of Mount Elgon and 26km (16 miles) northeast of Kitale is Saiwa Swamp National Park, Africa's smallest national park (being only 2km², or half a mile in size).

Saiwa was made a national park to protect a population of rare sitatunga antelope. It consists of a narrow swampy valley filled with rushes and sedges, bordered by a narrow band of riverine forest – an ideal habitat for the sitatunga which has evolved specially adapted hoofs to live in this environment. A nice feature of this park is that there are no roads, so visitors do all their viewing of animals and birds on foot.

Several observation towers have been built along the edge of the swamp to enable visitors to view the wonderful sitatunga, and other animals such as the De Brazza, Syke's and colobus monkeys, olive baboon, bushbuck, reedbuck, suni and otters.

Just north of Saiwa, the village of **Kapenguria** is renowned for the publicity it received in 1953 when Jomo Kenyatta was tried and convicted for his alleged role as head of the Mau-Mau movement.

Western Kenya at a Glance

BEST TIMES TO VISIT

To visit Masai Mara, almost any time is good, though heavy rains from end March to May, and again in November to early December, can make travel difficult. **July to September** normally coincides with the wildebeest migration. Rain can occur in any month at Lake Victoria, usually late afternoon.

GETTING THERE

Air Kenya operates daily scheduled flights to **Masai Mara** from Wilson Airport, tel: (02) 501601/2/3/4; or call Safari Air Services at tel: (02) 501211/2/3. To get to **Lake Victoria**, Kenya Airways has daily **flights** to Kisumu, tel: (02) 82288.

GETTING AROUND

There is a good (but busy) **road** from Nairobi to Kisumu. In **Masai Mara** all luxury tented camps and lodges have **four-wheel-drive** vehicles. To visit **Mfangano** and **Rusinga islands**, most visitors fly in from Masai Mara. You can also drive to Rusinga Island across a causeway from Mbita Point. Passenger boats run to Mfangano from Kisumu, via Homa Bay; cars can be parked at the district officer's office.

WHERE TO STAY

Masai Mara Reserve
Governors Camp: luxury tents on banks of Mara River, book through Musiara Ltd.

Little Governors Camp: small camp, beautiful setting, book through Musiara.
Kichwa Tembo Camp: built on edge of small riverine forest patch with sweeping views, book through Windsor Hotels International.
Siana Springs, outside reserve: luxury double tents, book through Windsor Hotels International.
Mara Serena Lodge, near Mara River: based on traditional Maasai architecture, book through Serena Lodges and Hotels.
Mara Safari Club: tented lodge on banks of Mara River, book through Lonrho Hotels.
Mara Intrepids in reserve: double tents on Talek River bank, book through Prestige Hotels Ltd.
Mara River Camp outside reserve: permanent tented camp (27 double tents) in beautiful spot on Mara River, write to PO Box 48019, Nairobi; tel: (02) 335935, fax: 216528.

ISLAND CAMPS
Mfangano Island Camp: beautiful, exclusively small lodge under giant figs in secluded bay, book through Musiara Ltd.

Rusinga Island Camp: three thatched-roof rondavels, book through Lonrho Hotels.

Lake Victoria
Homa Bay Hotel, Lake Victoria: modern, tel: (02) 229751 or 330820.
Sunset Hotel, Lake Victoria: overlooks lake, book through African Tours and Hotels.
Kericho Tea Hotel: historic colonial edifice, contact African Tours and Hotels Ltd.
Mount Elgon Lodge: book through Msafiri Inns.

USEFUL ADDRESSES

African Tours and Hotels, PO Box 30471, Nairobi; tel: (02) 336858, fax: 218109.
Lonrho Hotels, PO Box 58581, Nairobi; tel: (02) 216940, fax: 216796.
Msafiri Inns, PO Box 42013, Nairobi; tel: (02) 336858.
Musiara Ltd, PO Box 48217, Nairobi; tel: (02) 331871/1041, fax: 726427.
Prestige Hotels, PO Box 74888, Nairobi; tel: (02) 338084, fax: 217278.
Serena Lodges and Hotels, tel: (02) 725111, fax: 725184.
Windsor Hotels International, PO Box 74957, Nairobi; tel: (02) 219784, fax: 217498.

KISUMU	J	F	M	A	M	J	J	A	S	O	N	D
AVERAGE TEMP. °F	73	75	75	73	70	68	68	70	70	72	73	72
AVERAGE TEMP. °C	23	24	24	23	21	20	20	31	31	22	23	23
Hours of Sun Daily	9	9	8	8	8	8	7	7	7	8	8	9
RAINFALL in	3	4	5	7	7	6	4	3	3	4	5	4
RAINFALL mm	86	94	128	172	183	142	94	87	82	96	126	104
Days of Rainfall	7	10	11	17	13	8	7	8	8	10	13	9

4
Great Rift Valley

The **Great Rift Valley**, part of an immense fracture in the earth's crust running 6440km (4000 miles) from Jordan to Mozambique, slices through Kenya from north to south. One of the most impressive features on earth, its stretch through Kenya encompasses the most dramatic, spectacular and varied scenery, unsurpassed anywhere in Africa.

Several volcanoes, now mostly dormant, occur in the valley, although just over the border in Tanzania, one volcano, Lengai, is still very active. Kenya is successfully harnessing the potential of volcanic activity in a number of ways: steam jets issuing from the lower slopes of **Mount Longonot** in **Hell's Gate National Park** power turbines which now produce approximately one-fifth of Kenya's power requirements. To the east of Longonot, at the top of the escarpment, carbon dioxide gas seeping to the earth's surface is further evidence of volcanic activity; the gas is collected, compressed into a liquid state and bottled. It is also made into dry ice for refrigeration.

The Great Rift Valley can be both inhospitable, with its gruelling lava terrain, searing temperatures and seething hot springs; and life-nurturing, with its rich, arable farmlands yielding coffee, fruit and other edible products.

Another distinctive feature is its large number of alkaline lakes, all very different and some, such as **Nakuru** and **Bogoria**, famous for the breathtaking sight of their pink flamingos; world-famous American ornithologist, Roger Tory Peterson, described Nakuru as 'the world's most fabulous bird spectacle'.

CLIMATE

The Rift Valley can be visited year-round, bearing in mind the **rainy season** (March to May), followed by rain again in November. Around Lakes Nakuru, Elmenteita and Naivasha, the weather often turns **cloudy** in the afternoon, followed by a rain shower. Temperatures vary considerably, mostly depending on altitude. At the higher altitudes, nighttime temperatures can drop below 10°C (50°F).

Opposite: *flamingos feeding at Lake Bogoria.*

DON'T MISS

*** Flamingos at Lake
Nakuru or Lake Bogoria
*** A visit to Lake Naivasha,
most beautiful of the lakes
*** A stay at Lake Baringo's
Island Camp
** A climb up Mt Longonot,
Kenya's youngest volcano
** Night game-viewing at
Delamere camp.

GREAT RIFT VALLEY

Although still not fully understood, the Rift Valley was initially formed two million years ago when continental drift was taking place. Violent subterranean forces prised the earth's crust apart, causing the collapse of the land between parallel fault-lines. A Scottish geologist, John Walter Gregory, was the first to recognize the Rift Valley; he came across it in 1893, at a spot near **Lake Naivasha**, but because of trouble with the Maasai, Gregory moved on northwards to **Lake Baringo**. Here he took samples of rock from the valley floor and from the top of the surrounding escarpments, and found them to be similar. It

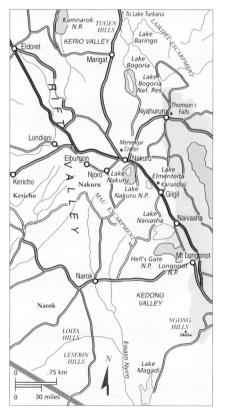

was he who named his discovery the Rift; although there are other similar rifts in the world, Gregory believed this to be the greatest, and it became known as the 'Great Rift Valley.'

Where the Rift Valley enters Kenya, the floor lies at an altitude of 198m (650ft), with little sign of steep escarpments, but at Lake Baringo to the south, the valley rises to 914m (3000ft) and is just over 16km (10 miles) wide; to either side, spectacular escarpments rise several thousand kilometres. The valley floor continues to rise until it reaches just over 1829m (6000ft) in the central highlands, before dropping down again to **Lake Magadi**, on the border with Tanzania.

Lake Turkana

Of the Rift Valley's lakes, Lake Turkana (formerly Lake Rudolf) in the extreme north is the most dramatic. With a length of 318km (198 miles) and a width of around 56km (35 miles), it's one of the largest alkaline lakes in the world.

Count Samuel Teleki von Szek, a Hungarian sportsman, geographer and wildlife enthusiast, and his companion Lieutenant Ludwig von Höhnel, first discovered Lake Turkana in 1887, naming it Lake Rudolf in honour of Crown Prince Rudolf, heir to the Austro-Hungarian empire, a man who had taken great interest in their expedition. At the time the lake was known to the local people as *Basso Narok* (black lake).

Turkana, often referred to as the 'jade sea' because of the blue-green, jade-like colour of its water, is surrounded by harsh, rugged, dry desert country with spectacular scenery that's almost constantly whipped by strong winds. The lake's waters are only slightly alkaline (the water is drinkable), and as a result support some aquatic vegetation and a large population of fish and birds, as well as crocodiles which prey on them. Huge Nile perch – some as large as 90kg (200lb) – occur in the waters, proving that at one time the lake was connected to the Nile system. Tigerfish and tilapia species are also present in the lake.

EL-MOLO TRIBE

The el-Molo, Cushitic people living along the southeastern corner of Lake Turkana's shore and once believed to be a dying race, now exceed 500 in number as a result of intermarriage with the Turkana and Samburu peoples, and access to medical help from a nearby mission station. Through this intermarriage, however, their tribal language is disappearing.

Unfortunately the lake's level has dropped quite dramatically. The reason is that the two major rivers flowing into the lake, the Omo (running into the lake's northern end from Ethiopia) and the Turkwel (entering the lake on the western shore) have both been dammed for irrigation and hydroelectric schemes. Added to this is the fact that for a number of years now, rainfall in the northeast has been very poor and irregular. Ferguson's Gulf, a shallow bay of water which was thought to be an important breeding area for fish, has for some years been totally dry, leaving the **Lake Turkana Fishing Lodge** stranded and the nearby fish-processing plant, built by the Norwegians, redundant.

Below: *an elaborately beaded Turkana girl.*

Sibiloi National Park **

Covering an area of 1570km² (600 sq miles) the Sibiloi National Park has a surprising number and variety of wildlife, despite its being

SIGNS OF PREHISTORIC MAN

Around Lake Turkana's shores is abundant evidence of prehistoric animals and ancient man: a part of the eastern shore has revealed traces of man and his predecessors going back 3 million years, and is referred to as the 'cradle of mankind'. The area, known as **Koobi Fora**, is now protected and forms part of **Sibiloi National Park**. The park's headquarters here house a museum where some of the fossils are displayed. It's possible to visit the nearby sites if you gain permission from the National Museum in Nairobi.

Below: *Lake Turkana and its volcanic South Island.*

extremely arid and windblown. It includes lion, Grevy's zebra, beisa oryx, gerenuk, Grant's gazelle and a unique family member of the topi, called tiang.

Birdlife, too, is varied and at times plentiful, especially during the European winter months, when the lake shore is home to large numbers of wading birds, among them black-tailed godwits and redshanks. For the really keen bird-watcher, the birds found in the arid bush are perhaps the most interesting: swallow-tailed kites, Heuglin's and kori bustards, Lichtenstein's sandgrouse, Somali and carmine bee-eaters and both crested and short-crested larks are just a few of the wonderful birds found in this area.

Turkana's Volcanic Islands

Lake Turkana has three islands, all of them volcanic. **North Island**, small and rocky, is inhabited only by snakes. Midway down the lake is **Central Island** – a national park – formed from three still-active volcanoes which occasionally belch out steam and smoke. Each of the volcanoes is flooded; the result, three interesting

lakes which serve as breeding grounds for possibly the world's largest crocodile population. The lakes are named after their most prominent features: Crocodile, Flamingo and Tilapia. The third island, appropriately named **South Island**, is the largest; it is also a national park. Volcanic ash covers most of it, making it most desolate except for a few feral goats. At night its volcanic vents often glow, and have inspired the el-Molo people to relate stories of evil spirits.

Few people visit Turkana's southern shore, an area of scorched, black lava and one of the most inhospitable places on earth. The shoreline is dominated by **Teleki's Volcano** and **Nabuyatom Cone**, which form part of 'The Barrier' separating Turkana from the Suguta Valley, one of the world's hottest locations: midday temperatures average between 72–77°C (130–140°F). The terrain is so difficult that there is virtually no access between the east and west shores. The least known of the Rift Valley lakes, **Lake Logipe**, lies in the Suguta Valley; it can, at times, rival famous Lake Nakuru with spectacular numbers of flamingos.

Mention must be made of **Mount Kulal**, which has been designated an International Biosphere Reserve – one of three such reserves in Kenya. Mount Kulal's cool, forested slopes, rising to 2416m (7927ft) just a few short miles from Turkana's sunbaked southeastern shore, are an incredible contrast. A fascinating mountain with two peaks separated by a deep gorge and a knife-edge ridge, Kulal is the main cause of the very strong winds that are such a feature in this area. The winds usually start to blow during the late morning, slowly becoming stronger until by nightfall they are almost gale force; they suddenly cease before dawn.

Above: *a 'rock desert' of lava near Lake Turkana.*

A MODERN MYSTERY

Lake Turkana's el-Molo people are known to weave their stories of intrigue around the hiss of the island volcanoes, but a real mystery did occur on South Island in 1934. At that time, Vivien Fuchs (later 'Sir') of Antarctic fame led an expedition to the island, returning to the mainland after three days, from where he sent another member to join the colleagues he'd left behind. However, neither man nor trace was ever seen again, and their disappearance has yet to be satisfactorily explained.

Below: *bougainvillea festoons the grounds of the Lake Baringo clubhouse.*

Lake Baringo ★★★

Continuing southwards along the Rift Valley is Lake Baringo, a freshwater lake and now a major tourist resort lying deep in the valley.

Although surrounded by semidesert, the scenery is rugged and majestic. To the east of the lake rise the dramatic Tugen Hills, birthplace of President Moi, and to the west is the Laikipia Escarpment. Unfortunately the lake's waters are stained brown: considerable overgrazing by goats has stripped the soil of its groundcover, and during heavy rains, the fine volcanic silts are washed into the lake. They are so fine that much of the silt never settles, resulting in murky water. Even so, the lake holds a good fish population – mainly tilapia and barbel – plus herds of hippo and many crocodile.

Lake Baringo's water is fresh, in spite of there being no obvious outlet. When Gregory explored the lake in 1893, he concluded that Baringo was at one time connected to Lake Turkana, but that volcanic activity had lifted the northern end of the lake, cutting off its outlet. It is believed today that the outlet lies submerged; 50km (31 miles) north of Baringo, at Kapedo in the middle of

hot, dry, barren country, is an oasis of doum palms with hot springs and a 9m (30ft) waterfall: this is believed to be Lake Baringo's outlet.

Nowadays, Baringo is regarded as the bird-watching centre of Kenya, with over 450 species recorded. Not only is there a proliferation of waterbirds, but there is also a wonderful variety of birds in the acacia bush bordering the lake, many of them difficult to see elsewhere. Whether you are a bird-watcher or not, an early morning walk here should really not be missed.

Other activities at Lake Baringo are fishing (tilapia, barbel, catfish), water-skiing and wind-surfing; facilities and hiring equipment are available at Island Camp.

Njemps People

The Njemps, numbering less than 9000, are related to both the Maasai and the Samburu, but have become sedentary rather than nomadic. Although the Njemps own cattle and goats, because of the harsh climate they rely heavily on fishing, mostly from small canoes, for their livelihood. These canoes are sometimes used to carry sheep and goats over considerable distances to other islands, where they can forage for food; the image of a solitary Njemps fisherman slowly paddling his craft across the water is a distinctive and lasting one.

FISHING FOR A LIVING

The unique canoes used by the Njemps tribe are made from ambach, a lightweight wood which grows around the lake shore. Lengths are bound together – traditionally with wild sisal but increasingly with nylon cords – into a peaked bow and open stern. A separate deck of ambach is then constructed to fit into the bottom of the canoe, where the fisherman sits. This flimsy but buoyant vessel is propelled by small hand paddles which look inefficient but appear to work well for the fishermen. They also fish standing in the water, often with crocodile nearby; but it's an almost unheard of occurrence that a person has been attacked by one, presumably because the predators are so well fed!

Top left: *a young Njemps boy paddles his lightweight canoe over the placid waters of Lake Baringo. His people have much in common with the Maasai.*

Below: *a jetting geyser shrouds Bogoria's lake shore in steam.*

Even though the Njemps cultivate, eat fish and have abandoned the *manyatta* tradition (young warriors living in separate groups), Maasai cultural traits remain dominant. They dress and decorate themselves in the Maasai fashion, their songs and dances are similar, and they practise circumcision and retain the warrior system.

Lake Bogoria ★★★

Just south of Baringo is Lake Bogoria (formerly known as Lake Hannington); the lake and surrounding area is a national reserve. Lying close to the base of the Ngendalel Escarpment, which rises 610m (2000ft) above the lake, Bogoria is scenically the most spectacular and dramatic of all the Rift Valley lakes. Long, narrow, and deep, it is strongly alkaline and surrounded by dense, impenetrable thorn bush. Around the lake shore are a number of geysers and hot springs, which at dawn can sometimes form a thick mist. When one stands near one of the geysers and peers across the lake through the clouds of hot swirling steam to the towering wall of the escarpment, it is easy to imagine how the earth split apart to form the dramatic, chiselled sweep of the Rift Valley.

There are times when Lake Bogoria is home to thousands of flamingos; to watch skeins of them flying along the lake towards the geysers and hot springs where they drink and bathe is a wondrous sight not easy to forget. John Walter Gregory, when he visited the lake during his explorations, called it 'the most beautiful sight in Africa.'

Above: *a jackal and a young waterbuck on the shore of Lake Nakuru.*

During some years, lesser flamingos build their cone-shaped mud nests at Bogoria, and though they occasionally lay eggs, they strangely have never been known to breed there. Bogoria is also home to a variety of mammals: common zebra, Grant's gazelle, impala, klipspringer, dik-dik and the magnificent greater kudu, which is both prolific and tame.

Lake Nakuru ★★★

Across the equator, southwards of Bogoria, lies the Rift Valley's most famous lake, Nakuru. Known all over the world for its flamingos, it is also alkaline and is recognized as being one of the natural wonders of the world.

In 1961, the southern two-thirds of the lake was established as a sanctuary to protect the flamingos, and in 1967 Nakuru was declared a national park, the first one in Africa to be set aside for the preservation of birdlife. The park's area was extended in 1969 to encompass the whole lake, and since then has been extended once more; it now covers an area of 188km² (73 sq miles).

Lake Nakuru is now also a rhino sanctuary, harbouring a population of over 30 black and two white rhino; but the flamingos, of course, have always been the main attraction. At times there may be almost two million

---

RIFT VALLEY VOLCANOES

The length of the Rift Valley is studded with volcanoes varying in age, size and shape. Some of them have the classical cone shape (Mt Longonot is a good example), while other much older ones can sometimes be difficult to identify as volcanoes, because the original crater has been eroded away with time and only the hard central plug remains. Examples of these, starting in the north of the country, are: North, Central and South islands in Lake Turkana, Teleki's Volcano, Kakorinyo, Silali, Londiani, Menengai, Eburru, Longonot, Suswa, Olorgesailie, and Shomboli on the Tanzanian border.

flamingos in residence, forming a stunningly beautiful deep-pink band around the edges of the lake shore.

During 1960 a small fish which is tolerant to alkaline water, *Tilapia grahami*, was introduced into the lake to control mosquito larvae. These tilapia have since multiplied both in number and in size, attracting lots of fish-eating birds such as pelicans, cormorants and herons. Although over 400 species of bird have been recorded at Nakuru, they are not the only attraction the lake has to offer; over 50 species of mammal have been recorded and it is perhaps the best place in Kenya to see leopard.

Some years ago a number of endangered Rothschild's giraffe was translocated here; they have multiplied and are now a common sight.

Troops of black-and-white colobus monkeys can be seen in the yellow-barked acacias (*Acacia xanthophloea*) in the southern part of the sanctuary. This is also a good area to see the magnificent crowned eagle, Africa's most powerful. Along the eastern shore of the lake stretches a magnificent forest of tree euphorbias (*Euphorbia candelabrum*), unique in Kenya. It is, in fact, the largest single euphorbia forest in Africa.

FLAMINGOS

Two flamingo species occur on most of the Rift Valley lakes: the greater and the lesser flamingo, the latter outnumbering the former by 200 to one. Although they frequent the lakes that are alkaline, they use any fresh-water source flowing into the lake, and hot springs that are not strongly alkaline, for bathing and drinking. What makes these birds so attractive is the deep coral hue of their legs and beaks, and their salmon-pink plumage. During courtship displays, flamingos will open their wings to reveal the vibrant colour underneath.

Lake Elmenteita **

Smallest of all of the Rift Valley's lakes is Lake Elmenteita; shallow and alkaline, it has two small seasonal rivers flowing into it. The lake is surrounded by an almost lunar-like landscape of extinct volcanoes and lava flows; it is also very attractive, its water often edged with pink flamingos.

Elmenteita lies on Soysambu Estate, owned by Lord Delamere whose father was one of the early settlers in Kenya. The estate, which still harbours good numbers as well as a variety of game, is now the **Soysambu Wildlife Sanctuary**, complete with a luxury permanent tented camp. Only visitors staying at the camp, however, are permitted to visit the sanctuary.

On the western side of the lake is a number of secluded bays with small lava islands, which were, for several years, used by greater flamingos as a nesting site. Although flamingos usually make their nests out of mud, at Lake Elmenteita they would lay their eggs on the lava, only adding a few pieces of grass. However, for a number of years now these islands have been taken over by white pelicans, Kenya's only breeding colony. Because Elmenteita has no fish, the pelicans have to commute to nearby Lakes Nakuru and Naivasha to obtain their food.

Opposite: *spoonbills crowd the shoreline of Naivasha, the highest and purest of the Rift Valley's lakes. The waters are home to more than 400 bird species.* **Below:** *the black-and-white colobus, a prominent resident of the forests.*

To the south of the lake is **Eburru**, an old volcano which has at least 200 steam jets around its base. These jets are an important source of fresh water in the area, obtained by condensing the steam.

Nearby is **Kariandusi**, a prehistoric site first worked on by Dr Louis Leakey in 1928. There is also a mine here, where diatomite (deposits of ancient microscopic aquatic organisms) is extracted. Diatomite is used for water filters in industry.

Above: *part of the grace-fully embowered grounds of the Lake Naivasha Country Club, to the west of the once notorious aristocratic playground of 'Happy Valley'.*

Opposite: *The waters of Lake Naivasha are too chilly for crocodiles, but hippos seem to find them congenial enough.*

The 'Happy Valley' Set

The infamous 'Happy Valley' is an area between the western slopes of the Aberdares and the town of **Gilgil**, but the real centre used to be along the **Wanjohi River**. It is a beautiful, wide, grassy valley set at the foot of the Aberdares and looking out over the Rift Valley.

Soon after World War I a number of titled and aristocratic Euorpeans settled here. The first of these was Josslyn Hay (later Lord Erroll) who eloped to Kenya from England with Lady Idina Gordon; the scandal of their affair forced them to leave England in April 1924. Idina was eight years older than Hay and twice married.

Thus was Kenya's reputation launched as a place beyond society's official censure. There were soon stories of wild champagne and wife-swapping parties, endless orgies and drug abuse (cocaine and morphine).

These early settlers built themselves wonderful homes and were soon receiving European visitors with a taste for gambling and promiscuity. It was around this time that the area became known as 'Happy Valley', a term probably given to it by the London gossip columns; and it was here that the saying, 'Are you married, or do you live in Kenya?' originated.

Lake Naivasha ★★★

Lake Naivasha is the highest and the most beautiful of the Rift Valley lakes. At 1910m (6200ft), the water is fresh and the lake is fringed with dense clumps of papyrus (ancient Egyptians once used this to make paper). Kingfishers use the papyrus as a perch, and herons hide in it while searching for food.

Dominating Naivasha (known by the Maasai as *En-aiposha* – 'heaving' or 'to and fro' – a reference to how turbulent Naivasha can get in the afternoon) is **Mount Longonot**, a dormant volcano, while **Crescent Island**, at the lake's southern end, is part of the rim of an ancient submerged volcano. The island is a private game sanctuary open to visitors, who may walk among the game (there are no cats or dangerous animals).

Naivasha is yet another area popular for bird-watching (over 400 species have been recorded). It is also a favourite weekend retreat for Nairobi residents, who come here to sail, water-ski and fish. There are no crocodile in the lake as the water is too cold for them due to altitude, but there is a number of hippo. Early settlers introduced tilapia and later, black bass to control its increasing numbers. Both of these fish are preyed upon by one of the largest concentrations of fish eagle in Africa. Other not-so-popular introductions into the lake are Louisiana crayfish, which are thought to damage the fish, and the coypu, a South American rodent, which has eaten the beautiful water lilies; now floating weeds cover much of the surface. The lake's fresh water (it is assumed that Naivasha, like Baringo, has an underground outlet) is used extensively to irrigate

> **MOUNT LONGONOT**
>
> At 2776m (9108ft) Mount Longonot is the highest of the Rift Valley volcanoes. Visitors wishing to climb its crater should leave their car at the Longonot police station, although this means a walk of almost 7km (4 miles) to the start of the climb. The walk up to the crater's rim takes about four hours, and although very narrow, it is possible to walk around the entire rim. There is a track down to the crater floor, but beware of buffalo hiding in the thick scrub!

the richly fertile volcanic soils that exist in the surrounding areas. A variety of vegetables, fruit and flowers is grown, mostly for export, earning important foreign exchange.

Along the lake shore, vineyards produce grapes for the country's fledgling wine industry.

Lake Magadi **

The most southerly lake in Kenya's Rift Valley is Lake Magadi, a Maasai word meaning 'soda lake'. At an altitude of 579m (1900ft), Magadi is one of the world's most inhospitable lakes, a shimmering pink-coloured hellscape of overpowering heat and smell, with temperatures well over 38°C (100°F).

The lake is the second largest source of trona (sodium carbonate) in the world (the Salton Sea in the United States is the largest). Magadi differs from the other Rift Valley alkaline lakes in that its deposits well up from below the earth's surface. These deposits have been mined for the last 80 years by the Magadi Soda Company; production is now 220,000 tonnes annually, and the lake is still maintaining its enormous soda output. The trona is processed at Magadi into soda ash and sodium chloride (common salt); the soda ash is exported mainly to the Far East and Southeast Asia.

Although the vegetation around the lake is dry desert scrub, receiving only 380mm (15in) of rain in a good year, there is a surprising amount of wildlife. Giraffe, gerenuk, Grant's gazelle and wildebeest are all found here. Birdlife too can be spectacular, particularly near any of the hot springs: flamingo (thousands of lesser flamingos bred at the lake in 1962), pelican, stilt, avocet and the localized Magadi plover (chestnut-banded sand plover) are just a few of the many birds recorded in the area.

The Rift Valley's Flamingos

There is nothing more synonymous with the Rift Valley than its flamingos. These magnificent birds occur on all the valley lakes; although their favourite haunts are those that are strongly alkaline, they do occasionally occur in small numbers on the freshwater lakes. Both the lesser and the greater species are found in East Africa, the greater flamingo being a larger bird, the lesser occurring in larger numbers (it is believed there may be as many as four million lesser flamingo and somewhere between forty to fifty thousand of the greater species living on the lakes). It is not unusual to find 1.5 million resident at Lake Nakuru.

The two species do not compete with one another: greater flamingo feed mostly on aquatic invertebrates and crustacea in the mud on the lake bottom, while lesser flamingo feed almost exclusively on a blue-green alga called spirulina which hangs suspended in the top millimetre or so of the water. Flamingos' bills are adapted for this very specialized diet. The lesser flamingo's lower mandible, which lies uppermost when the head is bent over while feeding, is lightweight and acts as a float, keeping the bill at the optimum depth. Both mandibles are lined with fine bristly lamellae which act as filters, and the tongue is round, acting as a pump. Water is drawn into the bill through the action of the tongue, causing the laminae to lie flat. The water is not swallowed (the alkalinity makes it poisonous) but is pumped out again, at which the laminae stand erect, retaining the spirulina. The greater flamingo's bill is very similar but differs in that the laminae are fewer and much coarser.

FOOD FOR THOUGHT

It is estimated that each lesser flamingo eats 184g (6.5oz) of spirulina a day; this means that a million birds at Lake Nakuru consume around 184 tonnes in a single day – about 66,300 tonnes a year! Add to this figure an estimated 2550 tonnes of fish consumed by white pelicans – and it illustrates just how productive an alkaline lake such as Lake Nakuru can be.

Opposite: *a lone Maasai man crosses the inhospitable terrain around Lake Magadi. Despite the heat and harsh surrounds, the area sustains a surprising wealth of wildlife.*
Below: *flamingos in their thousands flock to the Rift Valley's lakes.*

Great Rift Valley at a Glance

BEST TIMES TO VISIT

Almost **any time of year** is suitable, but during rainy season, state of roads can make driving difficult, particularly in national parks and reserves.

GETTING THERE

Practically all Rift Valley areas south of Lake Baringo easily accessible by ordinary **saloon car**. Visitors to Lake Turkana and northern areas can make use of **Turkana Bus**, run by Safari Camp Services; converted four-wheel-drive Bedford trucks depart every week from Nairobi (this economically priced safari one of best ways to visit Turkana), contact Safari Camp Services, PO Box 44801, Nairobi; tel: (02) 228936.

WHERE TO EAT

Visitors to the Rift Valley are fully catered for at the lodges in which they are staying.

WHERE TO STAY

Lake Turkana
Oasis Lodge at Loiyengalani on lake's eastern shore: most comfortable lodge in the area, two pools fed by fresh water from a spring, write to PO Box 56707, Nairobi; tel: (02) 225255.

Lake Baringo
Island Camp, on Olkokwe Island in centre of lake: luxury permanent tented camp under shady acacias, wonderful views across lake and escarpment; occasional evening barbecues around pool very popular; book through Lonrho Hotels.
Lake Baringo Club, on lake shore near Kampi ya Samaki: rooms overlook lake across lawns where hippos graze at night; small but attractively sited pool; book through Block Hotels.

Lake Bogoria
Lake Bogoria Hotel near reserve's northern entrance gate at Loboi: first class, book through African Tours and Hotels.

Lake Nakuru
Lion Hill Lodge, on eastern shore: well-appointed rooms on steep hillside all have views over lake; sauna and pool; book through Sarova Hotels.
Lake Nakuru Lodge near southeastern corner of lake: good lake views; book through Let's Go Travel.

BUDGET ACCOMMODATION
Lake Turkana
Safari Camp Services, Loiyengalani: accommodation available at their base; also two campsites; write to PO Box 44801, Nairobi.
Lake Bogoria
Fig Tree Camp Site in reserve: most popular of a number of shaded campsites, enquire at reserve gate.
Lake Nakuru
Two public plus three private sites (need to be booked in advance by professional safari companies).

Lake Naivasha
Fisherman's Camp on lake shore: primarily campsite, but also number of self-catering *bandas* available, plus others on hillside overlooking lake; book through Let's Go Travel.

Lake Elmenteita
Delamere Camp on lake's northeast shore: small, exclusive permanent tented camp in Soysambu Wildlife Sanctuary (sanctuary open to Delamere Camp guests only); write to PO Box 48019, Nairobi, tel: (02) 335935, fax: 216528.

Lake Naivasha
Lake Naivasha Country Club (formerly The Lake Hotel) on lake shore opposite Crescent Island: set among yellow-barked acacias, green lawns and beautiful gardens, book through Block Hotels.
Loldia House, on Naivasha's north shore: old settler's house, part of group who own Govenors Camp, welcoming atmosphere, cuisine excellent; book through Musiara Ltd.
Safariland: hotel among beautiful gardens on lake shore; swimming pool; offers tennis, archery, horse riding; write to PO Box 72, Naivasha; tel: (0311) 20241.
Longonot Ranch House on Kedong Ranch, between Hell's Gate and Longonot national parks: colonial-style house overlooking Lake Naivasha; working cattle ranch with

Great Rift Valley at a Glance

abundant plains game; write to PO Box 48217, Nairobi; tel: (02) 332132, fax: 729508.

Mundui, home of Lord and Lady Cole: accommodation in large cottage near main house; set in private game reserve containing plains game and large variety of birds; book through Bush Homes of East Africa.

Elsamere, former home of Joy Adamson: small museum and research centre, accepts guests if rooms available and if they're members of conservation organization; write to PO Box 1497, Naivasha; tel: (0311) 30079.

Crater Lake Tented Camp: small camp on shore of Lake Songasoi (within ancient volcanic crater close to Lake Naivasha): six double tents; walks and ox-wagon safaris; book through Cordon Bleu Safaris.

TOURS AND EXCURSIONS

Bird-watching: resident naturalist at Lake Baringo Club organizes walks mornings and afternoons (morning walk along base of nearby cliffs highly recommended to bird-watchers and keen walkers); Baringo also runs bird-watching boat trips, although awnings restrict upward viewing; Delamere Camp has bird hides on the lake shore; escorted walks by Naivasha Country Club; vultures nest on cliffs of Hell's Gate gorge in Hell's Gate National Park, nearby Naivasha.

Boat trips: run by Island Camp (the Njemps act as excellent and knowledgeable guides); Lake Naivasha Country Club (includes visits to Crescent Island); Loldia House; and Safariland.

Game-viewing: Delamere Camp has a small tree house where guests can stay overnight to watch leopard attracted by bait; also on offer is a sundowner excursion to a cliff above the lake, and night game drives using powerful spotlights to view nocturnal animals, some rarely seen by visitors; Longonot Ranch House offers night game drives; plains game can be viewed in Hell's Gate National Park; Fischer's Column has a colony of hyrax, visitors permitted to walk around.

Horse riding: Loldia House and Longonot Ranch House have facilities for horse-riding enthusiasts.

Lake Excursions: Island Camp takes visitors to an Njemps village, where they can photograph the people; visits to other parts of Baringo, and nearby Lake Bogoria also available; Loldia House organizes visits to Hell's Gate and Nakuru national parks.

Photographic talks: Lake Baringo Club holds a pre-dinner slideshow and commentary on Lake Baringo's birds every evening, and shows a wildlife video after dinner.

Walking: guided walks arranged by Island Camp (using Njemps guides), Delamere Camp, Loldia House, and Longonot Ranch House.

Watersports: Island Camp has water-skiing and wind-surfing facilities; Loldia House offers fishing.

USEFUL ADDRESSES

African Tours and Hotels, PO Box 30471, Nairobi, tel: (02) 336858, fax: 218109.
Block Hotels, PO Box 47557, Nairobi, tel: (02) 335807.
Bush Homes of East Africa Ltd, PO Box 56923, Nairobi; tel: (02) 506139; fax: 502739.
Cordon Bleu Safaris, PO Box 70560, Nairobi; tel/fax: (02) 882634.
Let's Go Travel, PO Box 60342, Nairobi; tel: (02) 340331, fax: 336890.
Musiara Ltd, PO Box 48217, Nairobi; tel: (02) 331871/041.
Sarova Hotels, PO Box 30680, Nairobi; tel: (02) 333233.

NAKURU	J	F	M	A	M	J	J	A	S	O	N	D
AVERAGE TEMP. °F	64	66	65	63	63	62	62	62	61	61	61	62
AVERAGE TEMP. °C	18	19	18	17	17	16	16	16	16	16	16	17
Hours of Sun Daily	9	8	7	6	7	8	7	7	7	6	6	8
RAINFALL in	1	2	4	6	4	3	4	4	4	3	3	1
RAINFALL mm	34	38	90	160	110	67	95	88	110	59	63	30
Days of Rainfall	5	7	9	16	15	11	12	15	12	12	13	6

5
Northern and Eastern Kenya

This area, once known as Kenya's Northern Frontier District (NFD), is a vast expanse of hot semidesert terrain. It is a country of sand rivers whose courses are marked by clumps of doum palms, of rocky hills and isolated mountains which rise sheer out of the hot, dry plains. Two rivers flow through the area: the **Tana**, Kenya's longest river, which eventually flows into the Indian Ocean, and the **Ewaso Nyiro** which slowly disappears into the Lorian Swamp.

Northern and eastern Kenya are rich in mammal and bird species not found elsewhere, and fortunately there are a number of national parks and reserves to protect them. A group of nomadic tribes also lives in this difficult region – the Somali, Gabra and Samburu – herding camels, sheep and goats.

Most visitors to this part of Kenya are drawn by the **Samburu** and **Buffalo Springs** reserves. A special feature, too, is the practice by lodges within the reserves to attract leopard at night by placing bait in a tree across from the lodge. Powerful spotlights directed at the bait allow guests to watch this nocturnal animal at work.

The **Samburu** and **Samburu Serena** lodges also feed crocodiles, while guests look on. Staff at Buffalo Springs Lodge succeed in drawing the rarely seen African civet, and the occasional striped hyena, by putting out food at night close to the lounge.

It is better to visit these remote parts of Kenya with a reputable safari operator, who will always ensure that places considered unsafe will be completely avoided.

CLIMATE

This part of Kenya is **hot** and **dry** with an average temperature of 30°C (86°F); the average annual rainfall is about 350mm (14in). **April** and **May** experience the majority of the **rainfall**, and for the duration of November the rain returns once more.

Opposite: *the reticulated giraffe, resident of the northern region.*

DON'T MISS

*** Samburu and Buffalo
Springs reserves
*** Lewa Wildlife
Conservancy
** Meru National Park
** Shaba National Reserve
** Marsabit National Park.

Opposite, left: *a gerenuk
stands on its hind legs to
reach higher and more succulent leaves of an acacia.*
Opposite, right: *accommodation on stilts at the
Samburu Intrepids Camp.*

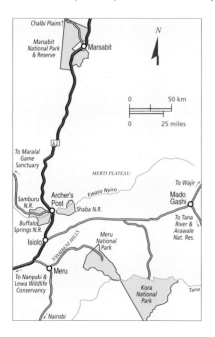

Samburu and Buffalo Springs National Reserves ***

These two small scenic reserves range in altitude from
800 to 1230m (2625 to 4036ft). They sit astride the Ewaso
Nyiro River (a Samburu name meaning 'river of brown
water') and are dominated by the sheer-walled **Ol
Lolokwe** and the rocky hills of Koitogor and Lolkoitoi.
The river, bordered by a green ribbon of riverine forest
made up mostly of tamarind trees, doum palms, Tana
River poplars, and the *Acacia elatior*, is the lifeblood of
this dry, arid region.

In the **Samburu National Reserve** north of the river, a
narrow plain quickly gives way to rocky hillsides which
are home to many leopard, while **Buffalo Springs
National Reserve** is mainly a rolling plain of volcanic
soils with dry riverbeds lined with doum palms.

The latter reserve has two small but important rivers
flowing through it: the Isiolo River which never dries up
(the Ewaso Nyiro occasionally does) and the Ngare
Mara. There are also the crystal clear
springs which give the reserve its
name. Unfortunately, their beauty has
been spoilt; one of the springs has had
an unsightly wall built around it and its
water piped to the nearby small town
of Archer's Post, while another has a
smaller wall around it and is used as a
swimming pool by campers. Fortunately, one small spring has been left
in its natural state and its waters flow
into the nearby Ewaso Nyiro River,
providing a magnet for wildlife.

Near Buffalo Springs is a wonderful
area called Champagne Ridge, covered
with flat-topped umbrella thorn trees
(*Acacia tortilis*) which are characteristic
of the area. On either side of the river
are extensive areas of salt bush (*Salsola
dendroides*), which few animals eat
because its leaves taste salty, but it does
provide cover for lion and cheetah.

It is the unique wildlife that attracts the many tourists to this wonderful area and, although there are no large spectacular herds, there is a wide variety. Four special mammals – gerenuk, Grevy's zebra, beisa oryx and reticulated giraffe – are all quite common and although there is some seasonal movement out of the reserves, you can usually count on seeing them. Other mammals include Burchell's zebra, buffalo, impala, common waterbuck, dik-dik (both Kirk's and Guenther's), Grant's gazelle, klipspringer, both greater and lesser kudu and warthog.

The highlight of any visit to Samburu and Buffalo Springs is to watch the large numbers of elephant – who are unperturbed by safari-goers – drinking and bathing in the shallow waters of the Ewaso Nyiro River. Crocodiles – some of them very large – and the occasional hippo are present in the river, although it is not an ideal environment for hippos as the dry bush to either side of the river provides them with very little food.

To the north of Samburu National Reserve is a forested range of mountains, **The Matthews**. A variety of game, including elephant, occurs in these mountain forests. The highest point, **Matthews Peak**, at 2375m (790ft) was named by Count Samuel Teleki in appreciation of help received on his expedition from Sir Lloyd Matthews, who was at the time commander-in-chief of the Sultan of Zanzibar's army.

THE GERENUK

This shy, graceful gazelle gets its name from the Somali language and means 'giraffe-necked', while its Swahili name *swara twiga* translates as gazelle-giraffe. Its outstanding characteristic features are long legs and a long, slender neck. The gerenuk's head is small for the animal's size; in front of the eyes are two preorbital glands which emit a tar-like substance that's deposited on twigs and bushes to mark the gazelle's territory. It feeds by standing erect on its hind legs, long neck stretched upwards, sometimes using its front leg to pull the vegetation down to an attainable level. Nibbling at such heights, it avoids competing with other gazelles and most antelopes. Gerenuks rarely drink water, obtaining all their moisture requirements from the food they eat.

Above: *visitors on a horseback safari in Lewa Wildlife Conservancy, south of Samburu National Reserve. The conservancy has had much success in protecting both black and white rhino.*

Camel Safaris in Samburu **

Camel safaris are a fairly recent innovation in Kenya and take place in Samburu country north of Nairobi. They are really walking safaris, where camels are used to carry all the equipment and food and, of course, an occasional tired walker. Guests are transported from Nairobi to a pick-up point deep in Samburu territory, where they meet their guide and the camels with their handlers, Samburu warriors wearing their traditional colourful clothes, which all adds to the mood of the occasion.

Walking is at a leisurely pace and the guide and Samburu warriors soon point out wildlife, including colourful birds, insects, flowers and interesting plants that most safari-goers miss. Although a variety of game is usually seen on this type of safari, one does not get as close to the game as on a conventional vehicle safari to a national park or reserve. Even so, the walk in the African bush with only the sounds of nature or the soft singing of your Samburu guides is something special. Each evening, camp is set up near a river or waterhole and guests have the choice of sleeping with only a mosquito net between them and the stars, or sleeping in a tent. Take the first option! You will never experience anything like it in your life! Food is prepared in the camp and tastes all the better when eaten outside under a big African night sky. These special safaris usually last from five to six days. For details of camel safaris, *see* p. 47.

Shaba National Reserve **

Although Shaba, lying to the east of the Samburu and Buffalo Springs reserves, is only separated from them by a major highway, it is a very different habitat. With an

---

A FLOWERING DESERT

In the thorn scrub and on many of the rocky outcrops grows the desert rose (*Adenium obesum*), whose colourful pink flowers are a beautiful contrast in this arid environment. Other common but interesting plants are the *Callalluma speciosa*, a succulent that produces balls of black flowers which give off a smell of rotten meat, thus attracting pollinating flies; the *Calotropis procera*, a tall plant with cabbage-like fleshy leaves that doesn't appear to be eaten by any mammal; and the red-flowering Erythrina trees, loved by sunbirds.

area of 280km² (108 sq miles), it is scenically dramatic; here the Ewaso Nyiro, instead of coursing through a plain, runs through deep gorges and waterfalls. **Mount Bodech** and **Shaba Hill** dominate the landscape, and the plains are dotted with springs, small swamps and rocky hills. The wildlife is similar to the other reserves, but generally not as plentiful.

Shaba is perhaps best known as the onetime home of author Joy Adamson who rehabilitated a leopard called Penny here. The story is told in Joy's book *Penny, Queen of Shaba*. It was at Shaba that Joy was murdered.

Lewa Wildlife Conservancy ★★★

South of Samburu is Lewa Downs, now called Lewa Wildlife Conservancy, owned by the Craig family. Originally a cattle ranch where wildlife was encouraged, it now carries an abundant and amazing variety, ranging from elephant and rhino to leopard and tiny dik-dik.

It is at Lewa that Anna Mertz, with the help of the Craigs, has established the **Ngare Sergoi Rhino Sanctuary**. Protecting both the black and white species, it is surrounded by an expensive solar-powered electric fence and is patrolled by armed game rangers – over 50 in all – equipped with radios. Recently the fence was extended to encircle the entire ranch area, a total distance of 35km (22 miles), and Lewa Downs was renamed.

LET LEWA BE YOUR HOST

Lewa Wildlife Conservancy offers accommodation in the form of three stone-built cottages next to the main ranch house. Each cottage has two rooms and a verandah with wonderful views over the surrounding countryside; another home is also available to guests. Meals are eaten with the Craig family, consisting mostly of fresh, home-grown ingredients. Plans are afoot to build a 30-bed lodge within the rhino sanctuary. Of interest on the ranch is a prehistoric site that has many Acheulian hand-axes strewn all around.

Left: *two elegantly beaded Samburu girls. The Samburu, a nomadic cattle-owning people, traditionally inhabit the northern region between Lake Turkana and the Ewaso Nyiro River.*

DOUM PALM

The doum palm, which can grow to 15m (49ft), is the only member of the palm family to have a divided trunk. The trees are riparian, occurring along the coast and in the arid areas of northern and eastern Kenya along seasonal river courses. Their fruit is much prized by animals, particularly baboon and elephant; humans occasionally eat it too. Elephants swallow the seeds whole, thus distributing them over large areas. Local people carve the seeds into buttons and other decorative items, which can look remarkably like ivory. The palm's sap is used to make a coarse alcoholic drink, the leaves for covering traditional huts, and for weaving baskets and mats.

There is now a total of 21 black and 11 white rhino in the conservancy, with the figure slowly rising as the population increases naturally. Cattle and sheep are still raised on the ranch, their numbers varying depending on the seasons. Wildlife includes greater kudu, reticulated giraffe, eland, hartebeest (a Mount Kenya subspecies), both Grevy's and common zebra, gerenuk, impala, Grant's gazelle, bushbuck and buffalo.

One of the main attractions of a stay at Lewa is being able to walk or ride on horseback among the wildlife. It is also one of the few places in Kenya which runs night game drives using powerful spotlights.

Meru National Park ***

To the east of Samburu, Buffalo Springs and Shaba lie the Nyambeni Hills, and beyond them is Meru National Park. The approach to Meru by road is quite dramatic; the road winds its way through the hills, a very densely populated area, and through coffee and tea plantations, and groves of miraa trees (*Catha edulis*). The leaves of this tree are chewed as a mild stimulant, which is exported to Somalia where it is known as *khat*.

The scenery changes dramatically as the road descends in altitude and suddenly one is in wild, remote country. Meru National Park was first gazetted in 1966 by the local council – the first African council to do so. The park covers an area of 870km² (335 sq miles); rainfall varies greatly, most falling in the western area and slowly decreasing eastwards.

Meru was made famous by the book and film *Born Free*, a story about the lives of Joy and George Adamson and Elsa, the lioness. Joy also reared a cheetah called Pippa here, which became the subject of another book titled *The Spotted Sphinx*.

Meru National Park is still an area of unspoilt wilderness, and despite its good network of well-maintained roads, it instils the feeling of real Africa. The park's attraction lies in the diversity of its scenery, and its wide variety of habitats ranging from forest, dry bush and grasslands to swamps and numerous rivers which are lined with doum palms, tamarind trees and various acacias. The Rojewero River, roughly bisecting the park, is the most beautiful. Along its banks, bird-watchers should look out for the rarely seen Peter's finfoot and the unusual palm-nut vulture.

Meru's wildlife, although not as approachable as in the more visited parks, is varied and often numerous. Lion, leopard and cheetah are usually sighted, as well as elephant and buffalo; hippo and crocodile are plentiful

Ewaso Nyiro River.
Opposite: *a group of Grevy's zebra in the Samburu National Reserve.*
Above: *the Meru's attractive Adamson's Falls.*

THE SINGING WELLS

Near Marsabit are the famous Singing Wells, dug by the Boran people who herd camels, cattle, sheep and goats. The men descend into the wells – many as deep as 15m (50ft) – and form a human chain to pass water in buckets, made out of giraffe skin, to one another. The water is poured into troughs where the livestock are waiting to drink. The name originates from the singing of the men as they pass the buckets along, helping them keep up a steady rhythm.

in the river. Burchell's and Grevy's zebra occur, as do reticulated giraffe, gerenuk and a number of antelope.

The Tana River forms Meru's southern boundary and it is here that the Adamson's Falls are located; they are named after George Adamson, whose final home was across the river in the **Kora National Reserve**.

Kora National Reserve

Kora National Reserve consists of inhospitable, dry acacia thorn bush, interspersed with granite kopjes. Between 1983 and 1984 a joint expedition of the National Museums of Kenya and The Royal Geographical Society studied this little known area, which proved to be a remarkable ecosystem virtually untouched by man. The book *Islands in the Bush* written by the expedition's leader, Malcolm Coe, records their findings.

It was in the Kora reserve that George Adamson, from 1970 onwards, made his final home. Still rehabilitating lions to the wild up to the time of his death, he was gunned down and murdered on 20 August 1989 by poachers.

Unfortunately there are virtually no roads or tracks in the reserve but the Kenya Wildlife Service has plans to build a bridge across the Tana from Meru National Park, and then open up Kora National Reserve to visitors.

Tana River National Reserve

The **Tana River** and **Arawale** national reserves are two little known and seldom visited wildlife areas on the river Tana, both more accessible from Malindi on Kenya's north coast (they lie 160km, or 99 miles, and 130km, or 80 miles, respectively north of Malindi). The Tana River National Reserve was established principally to protect two endemic primates, the red colobus and the crested mangabey. These monkeys occur nowhere else in East Africa and are threatened mostly by a decrease in habitat caused by man. Besides the seven different primates in the reserve, other mammals to be seen are elephant, lion, giraffe, common waterbuck, lesser kudu, hippo and crocodile.

Kenya's only herd of rare Hunter's hartebeest occurs in the dry thorn bush of the Arawale National Reserve. No visitor facilities exist – not even a gate!

Marsabit National Park and Reserve ★★

Also a little visited refuge, this reserve covers a total area of 1555km² (600 sq miles). Marsabit Mountain (meaning 'place of cold') is a cool, forested oasis rising out of the hot, dry **Chalbi Desert** plains. The thickly wooded slopes contrast sharply with the desert landscape, and the difference in temperatures causes thick mists to form each evening, which do not clear until early afternoon. These mists provide Marsabit's forests with moisture.

The park is studded with volcanic craters, the largest being **Got Bongoti**, and many are filled with fresh water. The best known, **Lake Paradise**, was home to Osa and Martin Johnson for four years where, in the 1920s, they made some of the world's first wildlife films.

Although difficult to see, wildlife is plentiful in the mountain forest: this includes a number of magnificent greater kudu, elephant, buffalo, reticulated giraffe and lion. The birdlife is good and it is probable that the rare lammergeyer, or bearded vulture, nests here.

Above: *the endearing and widely distributed little vervet monkey.*

Opposite: *Lake Paradise, one of a number of water-filled volcanic craters in the Marsabit park.*

AHMED, THE ELEPHANT

Marsabit National Park is perhaps best known as the home of Ahmed, a male elephant who was the proud owner of an enormous pair of tusks which touched the ground; President Jomo Kenyatta declared him a national monument, granting the impressive beast presidential protection until his death as a result of old age in 1974. Ahmed's body has been preserved and is on display in the Nairobi National Museum.

Maralal Game Sanctuary

On the northern edge of the Laikipia Plateau is the small town of Maralal, administrative centre of the Samburu District. A frontier town, it sits on the edge of a range of hills at an altitude of 1495m (4900ft) surrounded by beautiful cedar forests.

It was in Maralal that Jomo Kenyatta, Kenya's first president, was detained for a while by the colonial authorities. The house in which he was detained has been declared a national monument and is open to visitors. Two and a half kilometres (1.5 miles) out of town is the **Maralal Safari Lodge**, situated within the **Maralal Game Sanctuary**.

The lodge is mainly frequented by travellers on their way to or from Lake Turkana. It is set in the midst of a large forest glade near a waterhole which attracts large numbers of game such as the common zebra, eland, impala, buffalo and warthog. A short walk from the lodge is a hide where it's possible to see leopard, which are attracted to bait.

On the road to Turkana, 20km (12 miles) north of Maralal, is the **Lerogi Plateau viewpoint** with breath-taking vistas to the Rift Valley far below. The best time to experience this view is in the early morning.

Below: *the view across the Laikipia plateau. Below the escarpment is Lake Bogoria, a limpid, ice-blue sheet of water whose eastern shore is flanked by the 610m-high (2000ft) Siracho Cliffs. The lake, described by one early traveller as 'the most beautiful in Africa', is per-haps the one least known to tourists.*

Northern and Eastern Kenya at a Glance

Any time of the year; rain falls in March and in November, but during normal years is not heavy enough to make travel difficult or unpleasant.

As Samburu and Buffalo Springs reserves are remote and isolated, and in many places roads have been reduced to dirt tracks, visitors usually rely on **tours** organized by reputable safari companies.

Samburu National Reserve
Larsen's Tented Camp, on banks of Ewaso Nyiro River: tents raised on stilts, with good views over river; book through Block Hotels.
Samburu Intrepids Camp, upstream: similar to Larsen's, book through Prestige Hotels.
Samburu Lodge, on banks of Ewaso Nyiro River: large, modern safari lodge; leopard and crocodile attracted to bait every evening; book through Block Hotels.

Buffalo Springs National Reserve
Buffalo Springs Lodge, only one in reserve: near small permanent waterhole, striped hyena attracted to bait each evening; book through African Tours and Hotels Ltd.
Samburu Serena Lodge, on banks of Ewaso Nyiro: leopard and crocodile attracted to bait every evening; book through Serena Lodges and Hotels.

Shaba National Reserve
Shaba Sarova Lodge on banks of Ewaso Nyiro: amid oasis of sparkling springs, book through Sarova Hotels.
Kitich Camp in the Matthews mountains: permanent tents on banks of Ngeng River, book through Supoko Ltd.

Lewa Wildlife Conservancy
Lewa House: delightful farmhouse, six thatched-roof cottages; book through Bush Homes of East Africa.

Meru National Park
Meru Mulika Lodge: the original lodge, book through Msafiri Inns.
Leopard Rock Bandas: self-service *bandas*; book through AA Travel.
Kindani Camp at edge of Meru park: new lodge on river, thatched rondavels, contact Langwenda Safaris.

Tana River National Reserve
Research Camp: limited tent accommodation; contact National Museums of Kenya.

Marsabit National Park and Reserve
Marsabit Lodge in park: overlooks waterhole; book through Msafiri Inns.

Maralal Game Sanctuary
Maralal Safari Lodge at northern edge of Laikipia Plateau: write to Box 45155 Nairobi; tel: (02) 211124/5, fax: 214261.

AA Travel, PO Box 14982, Nairobi; tel: (02) 337900.
African Tours and Hotels Ltd, PO Box 30471, Nairobi; tel: (02) 336858, fax: 218109.
Block Hotels, PO Box 47557, Nairobi; tel: (02) 335807, fax: 340541.
Bush Homes of East Africa, PO Box 56923, Nairobi; tel: (02) 506193, fax: 502739.
Langwenda Safaris Ltd, PO Box 56118, Nairobi; tel: (02) 445797/4494, fax: 443267.
Msafiri Inns, PO Box 42013, Nairobi; tel: (02) 229751/3488, fax: 227815.
Prestige Hotels, PO Box 74888, Nairobi; tel: (02) 338084, fax: 217278.
Sarova Hotels Ltd, PO Box 30680, Nairobi; tel: (02) 333248, fax: 211472.
Serena Lodges and Hotels, PO Box 48690, Nairobi; tel: (02) 710511, fax: 718103.
Supoko Ltd, PO Box 14869, Nairobi; tel: (02) 444288, fax: 750533.

MERU	J	F	M	A	M	J	J	A	S	O	N	D
AVERAGE TEMP. °F	73	75	77	75	71	71	70	71	75	77	71	71
AVERAGE TEMP. °C	23	24	25	24	22	22	21	22	24	25	22	22
Hours of Sun Daily	8	8	8	7	8	7	6	6	7	8	6	7
RAINFALL in	3	1	5	11	3	0	0.5	0	0.5	5	13	5
RAINFALL mm	80	39	126	282	86	5	10	8	16	140	328	139
Days of Rainfall	7	6	8	17	10	3	3	3	4	9	17	12

6
Southern Kenya

Kenya's southern areas are the most popular. Most recognized, and made famous by the Hollywood movie moguls, the glistening snow-capped **Mount Kilimanjaro** dominates **Amboseli National Park**. At 5895m (19,341ft) it is Africa's highest mountain, and the first breathtaking view of its magnificent peak is one that stays with you forever. **Tsavo**, Kenya's largest national park cut through by the Nairobi–Mombasa highway, is famous for its magnificent wildlife and its quality lodges. Then there are the **Chyulu Hills** composed of gravelly lava soil, but with the onset of the rains a superficial cloak of green appears to transform the slopes into fragile but beautiful undulating grasslands.

Over the years, Amboseli has undergone a startling change in appearance: the swamps have increased dramatically in size and much of the beautiful acacia woodland has been destroyed. Theories abound as to the swamps' sudden expansion – underground movement, global warming and so on – but there is no doubt that Kilimanjaro's ice cap is receding. A contributing factor is the considerable clearing of forests on Kilimanjaro's slopes; water now runs off the mountain during heavy rains instead of the majority of it being absorbed. The destruction of the acacia woodlands has been blamed on the increase in the park's elephant population. Although this cannot be denied, the rising water table has brought mineral salts to the surface which are not tolerated by the trees, thus aiding their destruction. The parks do, however, have much to offer in terms of their wildlife.

CLIMATE

In southern Kenya it is generally **hot**, except for July and August which tend to be overcast. The more reliable **rains** fall during **November** (which is often cloudy) and December, but the main **rainy season** is actually from **March** to **May**.

Opposite: *elephants take to the road in the Amboseli National Park. Mount Kilimanjaro rises magnificently in the background.*

Amboseli National Park ***

Amboseli, situated due south of Nairobi, is Kenya's most visited wildlife area. Originally designated a reserve in 1948 and having an area of 3260km^2 (1259 sq miles), it was handed over to the Maasai in 1961, but because of conflict between the Maasai herds and the wildlife, the reserve was gazetted a national park in 1974 (at a fraction of its original size). Now 392km^2 (151 sq miles), the park centres on **Ol Tukai** (Maasai for the locally common phoenix palm), an area containing several swamps which are a magnet for wildlife.

To compensate the local Maasai who traditionally watered their livestock in this area, a number of wells were sunk in a spot outside the national park with funds donated by the New York Zoological Society.

Most of the park consists of a dry, ancient lake bed and fragile grasslands with patches of acacia woodland, while in the southern area there is a number of small, rocky, volcanic hills. Around the swamps – Ol Okenya, Ol Tukai and Enkongo Narok – the vegetation is lush with yellow-barked acacias and phoenix palms.

Despite its changing habitat, Amboseli National Park is possibly the best wildlife area in the whole of Africa to experience elephants at close range. Left unharassed by poachers, elephants feeding and bathing in the swamps must form the highlight of any safari.

Cynthia Moss and Joyce Pool, with their many assistants, have undertaken extensive

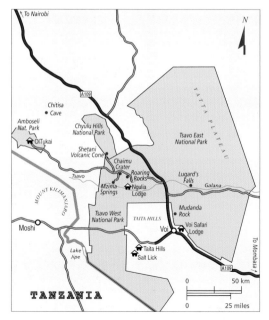

studies on these elephants; Cynthia herself has followed their movements for over 20 years, the most extended study of any one species by the same person in Africa.

Apart from elephant, the variety of game includes most species, from rhino, Masai giraffe, Grant's and Thomson's gazelle through lion, cheetah and leopard. In the drier areas of the park, away from the swamps, one can see fringe-eared oryx, gerenuk and eland. Birdlife is prolific too, especially in and around the many swampy areas. Both white and pink-backed pelicans, among many other waterbirds, share the open water areas with the beautiful pygmy goose which is quite uncommon in Kenya. Kingfishers and bee-eaters use the reeds along the swamps to look out for their quarry, and birds of prey are well represented, with the African fish eagle, martial eagle, pale chanting goshawk and the tiny pygmy falcon all occurring.

No visit to Amboseli is complete without a visit to Observation Hill, south of the airstrip. Walk to the top for a sweeping view over the whole of Amboseli spread out below. You will see the dust trails of animals walking across the expanses of dry plain to the water, and towards the south, an almost endless tract covered with acacias slowly merging into the base of Kilimanjaro.

Above: *the stone and cedarwood Amboseli Lodge, one of three venues within the Amboseli park. The area is famed for its elephants.*

ACCOMMODATION IN AMBOSELI

The national park has good lodges, as well as other forms of accommodation:

- **Amboseli Serena**, in the form of a Maasai dwelling
- **Amboseli Lodge**, fashioned from stone and cedar wood
- **Ol Tukai**, self-catering *bandas* with superb views.

Outside the park:
- **Tortilis Camp**, a new tented camp
- **Kimana** and **Kilimanjaro Buffalo** lodges; the latter, although some distance from the park boundary, has the best views of Mt Kilimanjaro.

Above: *Iltalal camp in the Chyulu Hills.*
Opposite: *a Grant's gazelle grazes in Meru National Park.*

Chyulu Hills National Park ★★★

The Chyulu Hills, lying to the east of Amboseli and running parallel with the main Nairobi to Mombasa road for 80km (50 miles), became a national park in 1983. The park comprises several hundred small, grass-covered volcanic hills that are only 400 to 500 years old, and a number of beautiful forested valleys. It is possible to walk along the crest of these hills, the highest of which is 4430m (14,535ft), from where the views of Kilimanjaro and the surrounding countryside are phenomenal. There is also a track through the hills, negotiable with a four-wheel-drive vehicle.

It is thought that rainfall percolating through the Chyulus, and so forming an underground river, feeds the famous Mzima Springs in nearby Tsavo National Park. A variety of wildlife, including the fringe-eared oryx, lives in this lovely area. Visitors wanting accommodation can choose between **Ol Donyo Wuas**, a small exclusive lodge, and **Iltalal Camp**, a permanent tented camp near the hills.

Immediately to the south of the Chyulus is a volcano named **Shetani** (the devil) whose black lava flows are only 200 years old, and the mighty Tsavo National Park.

TSAVO NATIONAL PARK

This very large national park immediately to the south of the Chyulu Hills is larger than Wales (and approximately the same size as the states of New Hampshire and Vermont combined). It has an area of 20,810km² (8035 sq miles) and varies in altitude from 230 to 2000m (755 to 6562ft). The main Nairobi to Mombasa road splits the park into two halves, **Tsavo East** and **Tsavo West**.

Although it was split mainly for administration purposes, the two areas differ remarkably. Tsavo East consists of miles of flat, dry thorn bush interspersed with magnificent baobab trees and dominated by the **Yatta Plateau**, the world's longest lava flow. In contrast, Tsavo West is much more scenic. Although it is also dry thornbush country interspersed with the occasional giant baobab, the vista is of volcanic mountains and hills, and outcrops with magnificent views. Along the **Tsavo River** the lush vegetation comprises doum palms, and tamarind and acacia trees.

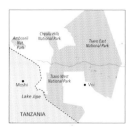

For much of the year Tsavo burns dry and dusty; the red Tsavo dust blankets everything – including the elephants, which are known here for their red colour. Once numbering tens of thousands, the drought and serious poaching of the late 70s and early 80s have severely reduced the elephant population (now around 5000). However, their destructive effect on the environment (*see* panel on p. 97) has been lessened as a result, and the vegetation is recovering, in many places thicker than before. After the rain, Tsavo transforms almost overnight; the grass pushes up fresh shoots and many wildflowers, such as the pink-and-white *Convolvulus*, quickly appear.

Both of the parks have an excellent network of well signposted tracks, which are generally well maintained.

SOME HORN FACTS

- The horns of all male antelopes (and many females) grow to various shapes, but never branch out to form antlers.
- Antelope horns are permanent, unlike a deer's antlers which are shed annually.
- Rothschild's giraffe males sometimes develop five horns (these are extra knobs that develop on the skull).
- Rhino horn is actually an outgrowth of the hide, composed of thickly compacted hair rather than bone.

Tsavo West National Park ★★★

Tsavo West is the most visited section in Tsavo National Park, offering many attractions apart from its wildlife. The foremost is the famous **Mzima Springs** where up to 227.3 million litres (50 million gallons) of cool crystal-clear water flow out of the ground through porous volcanic rocks. This water is believed to originate from the Chyulu Hills via an underground river. Water from

Above: *lava flow in the Tsavo area.*

Opposite: *rock strata in the Tsavo East park.*

the springs is piped all the way to the town of Mombasa on the east coast. At Mzima there is a car park and visitors are permitted to walk to the springs' source and along a pathway which follows the newly formed river. The walk is a wonderful experience; if you are quiet you may be rewarded with the sight of animals coming down to the water's edge to drink, and you are sure to see hippo clearly as they lie in the cool water.

One can also watch for them through the windows of an observation tank sunk into the river, which allows the visitor to enter a cool, new, underwater world. Close to the tank's windows are likely to be a number of fish, mostly barbel species. Troops of black-faced vervet monkeys and many very interesting birds inhabit the trees around Mzima. This is one of the few places where darters can be seen in Kenya.

Other interesting places to visit are the '**Roaring Rocks**', which get their name from the wind that hurtles through them. From here there are wonderful views over Tsavo from the top of a 98m (300ft) rock face; similar views can be experienced from the poachers' lookout. The volcanic **Chaimu Crater**, less than 200 years old and composed of black coke, is worth visiting and can be climbed if you are interested. This area is a good place to look out for klipspringer, a small antelope that's as agile as its Swahili name *mbuzi mawe* implies; that is, 'mountain goat'.

Besides the small but graceful lesser kudu, Tsavo's wildlife includes lion, leopard, cheetah, Masai giraffe, eland, fringe-eared oryx, buffalo, Burchell's zebra, yellow baboon, Coke's hartebeest and Grant's gazelle. Below **Ngulia Mountain** there is now a well-guarded rhino sanctuary containing a number of black rhino.

In the southwest corner of Tsavo West is **Lake Jipe**, 10km long and 3km wide (6 miles by 1.9 miles), which has the Kenya-Tanzania border running through it. Above the lake, the Tanzanian Pare Mountains form a dramatic backdrop, especially at sunset, and on clear days, Mount Kilimanjaro can be seen towards the north-west. Although there is a variety of game in the area, the birds attract most visitors. The lake shore is the best place in Kenya to see purple gallinules, black herons, pygmy geese, and occasionally lesser jacanas.

RED ELEPHANTS OF TSAVO
Tsavo's red elephants, at one time numbering around 50,000, have dramatically changed the vegetation in the area. During a very severe drought in the late 60s and early 70s, the elephants ate virtually all the vegetation and badly damaged many of the baobabs. Together with the black rhino, they died of starvation in large numbers and were the subject of much debate on the issue of culling, both in Kenya and the rest of Africa. This controversial subject is still under earnest discussion.

Tsavo East National Park **

Most of Tsavo East north of the Galana River is closed to the public; only a few professional safari companies are allowed to enter. The park has a good network of well-signposted tracks, and because the terrain is mostly dry, flat thorn scrub (the mountains and hills of Tsavo West are missing) and

BAOBAB TREE

The baobab (*Adensonia digitata*) is very common in both the Tsavo and Meru national parks, along the Kenyan coast, and inland in areas as high as 1250m (4100ft). For up to nine months of the year the trees, some of which may be 3000 years old, are leafless. Called *mbuyu* by the Swahili, the baobab features in the mythology of many African tribes who believe that God threw the tree out of his garden where it landed upside down, explaining its present-day 'uprooted' appearance.

Below: *view of the 300km (186 miles) Yatta Plateau – one of the world's longest lava flows – from Tsavo East's Voi Safari Lodge.*

there are fewer visitors, it has the aura of untamed Africa. The monotonous scrub is occasionally broken by green vegetation along one or other of the rivers that cross the area.

The most interesting section to visit is that around **Voi**, the park's headquarters. Dominated by the beautifully designed **Voi Safari Lodge** set high on a bluff, the Kandara swamp and Voi River lie to the east. The vegetation is rich along the river and it is here that most of the wildlife occurs. To the north of the lodge is **Mudanda Rock**, a miniature of Australia's Ayres Rock. Two kilometres (1.2 miles) long, it stands out prominently from the surrounding plains. Below the rock a natural waterhole attracts a great deal of wildlife at times. There is a parking area to the western side of the rock, and a footpath leads to a spot where one can climb up onto it. From here the views over the plains are wonderful, and occasionally one can see animals drinking.

Approximately 60km (37 miles) north of Voi are **Lugard's Falls** on the Galana River. Actually a series of rapids, the falls are most dramatic and impressive after rain, when the river's flow is constricted in the narrow, rocky gorge. Below the falls, very large crocodiles are usually to be seen at **Crocodile Point**.

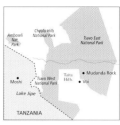

Left: *an ancient baobab –
the 'upside-down tree' of
African lore – rises above a
sisal plantation near the
town of Voi.*

Approximately 40km (25 miles) west of Voi is the 11,000ha (27,181 acres) **Taita Hills Game Sanctuary**, privately owned and run by the Hilton Hotel chain. This area was once an abandoned sisal plantation but has now been transformed into an exciting reserve containing a large variety of wildlife.

Nearby, the imposing craggy pinnacles of Taita's granite hills are impressive.

Lodge Luxury in Taita Hills

Taita Hills: Built to resemble a German fort, the small house is now a lodge, and is covered with a tangled mass of bougainvillea. `James Stewart's house', a small wooden structure built for the film *A Tale of Africa*, stands nearby and is open for tourists.

Salt Lick: Among the best in Kenya, this complex is architecturally based on the traditional Taita home – elephants browse unperturbed beneath the clusters of rondavels that are perched on stilts and linked by raised walkways. The lodge's waterhole attracts a wide variety of wildlife.

Both lodges must count among the world's most distinctive conference centres, set as they are in the midst of an array of African wildlife.

MAN-EATERS OF TSAVO

This is the title of a true account, written by Colonel J.H. Patterson, who was in charge of building a bridge over the Tsavo River for the Uganda Railway in 1898. For some time, workers were continually being dragged off into the night by two large male lions; the workers believed it was the Devil in the shape of a lion, as the mammals were quite fearless. Eventually, in December 1898, after the mounting toll included 28 Indian labourers and a large number of Africans, work on the bridge was brought to a halt until the lions were shot, the deed having been carried out by Colonel Patterson himself.

Southern Kenya at a Glance

This region experiences a warm climate **all year round**. The main rainy season is normally from the end of March to early May, and again in November when it is often cloudy during the day.

Amboseli National Park
The **roads** into and out of Amboseli are generally very **bad**, but at the time of writing the Emali to Kimana road was being rebuilt; this road gives access to the Lemeiboti gate on the northeast boundary of the park. Most of the **park's roads** are in fairly **good condition**, but a strong vehicle is still recommended. During heavy rain some areas of Amboseli are flooded.

Chyulu Hills
To enjoy the Chyulus, a **four-wheel-drive** vehicle is required. **Cars** can be **hired** in Nairobi and Mombasa; try The Car Hire Company in Nairobi, tel: (02) 225255, fax: 216553; or contact Galu Safaris in Mombasa, tel: (011) 229520/6, fax: 314226. The international airports and main hotels in Nairobi and Mombasa have Hertz representatives.

Tsavo National Park
Park **roads** are usually **excellent** – they are the best-maintained roads in any of Kenya's wildlife areas. A strong saloon car is suitable in normal conditions, but beware heavy rains, especially on tracks alongside the rivers.

Taita Hills Game Sanctuary
Roads in the sanctuary generally **good**; an ordinary saloon car is suitable.

Amboseli National Park
Amboseli Serena Lodge: built to represent Maasai dwelling, very pleasant and cool; has wonderful dining room and bar area; guest rooms a little small; unfortunately lodge does not face Kilimanjaro; book through Serena Hotels.
Amboseli Tortilis Camp: newly opened permanent tented camp; although outside park, very close to Kitirua gate; contact Cheli and Peacock, tel: (0154) 22551, fax: 22553.
Amboseli Lodge: large, noisy and busy, but faces Kilimanjaro; at time of writing main lodge was being enlarged and renovated; book through Kilimanjaro Safari Lodge.
Kilimanjaro Safari Club: also large, near Amboseli Lodge; rooms very close to each other, but afford wonderful views of Kilimanjaro; book through Kilimanjaro Safari Lodge.
Kilimanjaro Buffalo Lodge: outside national park (20–30 minute drive on dusty, often rough, road); has stunning views of Kilimanjaro; book through Kilimanjaro Safari Lodge.
Ol Tukai Lodge: Amboseli's first lodge, originally built for making of movie *Where No Vultures Fly*; is now self-catering; book through Let's Go Travel.

There are two camps and a lodge outside the park:
Kimana Lodge: book through Kilimanjaro Safari Lodge.
Kimana Leopard Camp and **Cottar's Kilimanjaro Camp**: book through Let's Go Travel.

Chyulu Hills
Ol Donyo Wuas: exclusive and small (eight guests), at foot of Chyulu Hills with wonderful views over surrounding countryside and on to Kilimanjaro; book through Richard Bonham Safaris.
Iltalal Camp: small permanent tented camp between Chyulus and Amboseli; book through Iain MacDonald Safaris Ltd.

Tsavo West National Park
Finch Hatton's Safari Camp: newly opened luxury permanent tented camp on banks of three spring-fed pools which feature hippo; 35 luxury tents raised on platforms facing pools; special views of Kilimanjaro from main building; old-fashioned, very high-class camp; book through Future Hotels.
Kilaguni Lodge: Kenya's first safari lodge (opened 1962);

Southern Kenya at a Glance

perfectly situated overlooking waterhole with magnificent views of Chyulu Hills and Kilimanjaro; during dinner the rarely seen striped hyena pays a visit; book through African Tours and Hotels Ltd.

Ngulia Lodge: spectacularly sited on top of rocky outcrop; waterhole in front of lodge is floodlit at night and each evening bait is put out close to open-sided dining room for leopard and ratel (the animals usually oblige); contact African Tours and Hotels.

Lake Jipe Safari Lodge: built a short distance from lake, has wonderful views of Kilimanjaro and North Pare mountains; write to the lodge at PO Box 31097, Nairobi; tel: (02) 227623, fax: 225508.

Tsavo East National Park

Tsavo Safari Camp on banks of Athi River: permanent tented camp, can only be reached by rubber dinghy; lovely relaxing spot with even a couple of tame fringe-eared oryx; book through Kiliman-jaro Safari Lodge.

Voi Safari Lodge: set high on rocky bluff overlooking water-hole and huge expanse of Tsavo, book through African Tours and Hotels.

Tiva River Camp on Tiva River: new permanent tented camp, offers walking safaris, book through Reachout Safaris.

BUDGET ACCOMMODATION
Ngulia and **Kitani** in Tsavo West offer two self-catering

lodges; book through Let's Go Travel.

Aruba Lodge in Tsavo East offers self-catering facilities, book through AA Travel.

Near the parks

Tsavo Inn on main Nairobi to Mombasa road, at Mtito Andei: small 30-room inn; book through Kilimanjaro Safari Lodge.

Crocodile Camp just outside national park near Sala gate on banks of Galana River: crocodiles attracted to bait at night; book through Repotel.

Taita Hills Wildlife Sanctuary

To reserve accommodation at any of the following com-plexes, book through Hilton International.

Taita Hills Lodge: impressive-looking, made out of sand-bags and built to resemble fortress; covered in climbing plants; also offers guided walks and balloon flights.

Salt Lick Safari Lodge: excellent night game-viewing lodge; rondavel-shaped rooms built on stilts overlooking series of waterholes

The Tents: small permanent tented camp in riverine forest along Bura River, 12 tents; in

centre of camp is James Stewart House, a wooden structure built over river.

AA Travel, PO Box 14892, Nairobi; tel: (02) 337900.

African Tours and Hotels Ltd, PO Box 30471, Nairobi; tel: (02) 336858, fax: 218109.

Future Hotels, PO Box 24423, Nairobi; tel: (02) 882744.

Hilton International, PO Box 30621, Nairobi; tel: (02) 332564, fax: 339462.

Iain MacDonald Safaris Ltd, PO Box 59224, Nairobi; tel: (02) 503265, fax: 506824.

Kilimanjaro Safari Lodge, PO Box 30138, Nairobi; tel: (02) 227136 or 337510, fax: 219982.

Let's Go Travel, PO Box 60342, Nairobi; tel: (02) 340331 or 213033, fax: 336890.

Reachout Safaris: PO Box 48019, Nairobi; tel: (02) 331191, fax: 216528.

Repotel, PO Box 46527, Nairobi; tel: (02) 227828.

Richard Bonham Safaris Ltd, PO Box 24133, Nairobi; tel: (02) 882521, fax: 882728.

Serena Hotels, PO Box 48690, Nairobi; tel: (02) 710511, fax: 718103.

VOI	J	F	M	A	M	J	J	A	S	O	N	D
AVERAGE TEMP. °F	79	79	81	79	77	73	72	72	73	77	77	77
AVERAGE TEMP. °C	26	26	27	26	25	23	22	22	23	25	25	25
Hours of Sun Daily	8	7	7	7	7	7	6	5	6	8	7	7
RAINFALL in	1	1	3	4	1	0	0	0	1	1	4	5
RAINFALL mm	36	32	76	94	34	8	6	10	18	30	102	130
Days of Rainfall	15	5	4	6	2	2	1	2	1	2	9	12

7
The Coral Coast

Mombasa is Kenya's second largest city and gate-way to East Africa. Over hundreds of years, Mombasa's harbour has seen a passing parade of fascinating creeds and cultures: Chinese junks, Arabian dhows, Portuguese galleons, merchant ships, passenger ships and cruise liners from all over the world.

Mombasa Town, an island that is now connected to the mainland by a causeway, was at war for centuries as the various conquerors in possession of the island throughout the years held authority over the coast and control of the hinterland. Fort Jesus, guarding the entrance to the Old Harbour, is a constant reminder of those fearful days. Mombasa's history goes back at least twelve centuries, at which time it was the residence of the people of Zeng, an African kingdom; it later became an Arab settlement. Both in 1505 and 1528, Mombasa was attacked by Portuguese galleons and sacked; in 1593 the Portuguese began to settle and started building Fort Jesus, where they remained until 1631 when they lost Mombasa in an Arab revolt. They briefly reclaimed the fort from 1632 to 1696, when the Arabs again took control. But for a brief occupation in 1728, the Portuguese finally left, leaving the Arabs in control until 1895, when the coastal strip became a protectorate of Britain.

Besides its historical heritage, Mombasa has miles and miles of white beaches to the north and south, holding a multitude of attractions: magical coral reefs sheltering beautiful tropical fish, an abundance of game fish for deep-sea anglers, and the chance to sail aboard a dhow.

CLIMATE

Temperatures generally are **moderated** by **sea breezes**, ranging from an average low of 24°C (75°F) in July to an average high of 28°C (82°F) in March. The heaviest rain usually falls in May, with rain again at the end of October and early November. The sea temperature is always warm and varies between 27–30°C (80–86°F) depending on the season. Humidity varies from 74% in February to 84% in May.

Opposite: *palm-graced Tiwi Beach on Kenya's south coast.*

DON'T MISS

*** Snorkelling off the Lamu
Archipelago
*** A ramble through Old
Mombasa town
*** Dining on the famous
Tamarind Dhow
*** *Son et lumière* show at
Fort Jesus
*** A trip to explore the
Gedi ruins
** A visit to Malindi resort.

OLD MOMBASA TOWN

The old town, hot and steamy, remains very much the same today as it was in the 19th century. Its narrow streets are lined with old Arab houses, many with traditional carved doors studded with brass, there are spice shops, coffee vendors and mosques, and dhows lying at anchor in the Old Harbour; although greatly reduced in numbers, they still ply their trade with various ports in Arabia as they have been doing for at least two thousand years. The dhows arrive, usually in early December on the northeast monsoon, with their traditional cargos of dates, dried kingfish and a few carpets and traditional chests. They leave eventually in the middle of May, at the latest, on the southeast monsoon with a cargo of *boriti* poles (mangrove), ghee and limes. Traditionally their main cargo would have been made up of slaves and ivory.

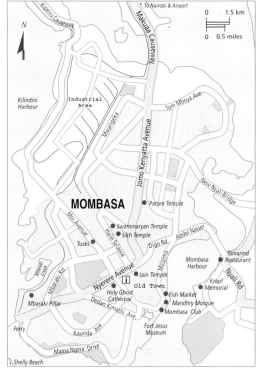

A Walk Through the Old Town ***

A good place to start is at **Fort Jesus**, which everyone should make an effort to visit. From the fort entrance, walk across the road, keeping **Mombasa Club** on your right, and on into Mbarak Hinaway Road. The shops along its length are now mainly filled with curios, but look out for shops selling spices and scents. You will pass **Mandhry Mosque**, Mombasa's oldest, built in 1570 (at one time there were almost 50 mosques in the Old Town

but today a little over 20 are still in use). You then reach **Government Square** and the **Old Harbour**, which have not changed much over the years. Here it is still possible to watch the loading of cargo onto the old trading dhows. After exploring Government Square and its interesting shops, turn into Thika Street and then left into Ndia Kuu which takes you back to the fort.

Above left: *Mombasa's Old Town, a place of mosques, spices and scents.* **Above:** *the cannons of Fort Jesus.*

Fort Jesus **

This 16th-century stronghold was built by the Portuguese to protect their trade routes to India. The architect was Italian, so the structure has all the features representative of an Italian fortress of the time. The fort, whose walls are 15m (50ft) high and 2.4m (8ft) thick, stands on an old coral ridge commanding the entrance to the Old Harbour.

At the end of the 17th century the Sultan of Oman sent an army to seize the fort; the siege lasted almost three years before finally falling into their hands. In 1728 the fort was recovered by the Portuguese without a struggle, but relinquished again later to remain under Arab rule until 1895 when Mombasa became a British protectorate. The fort was bombarded by the British Navy in 1878 and 1895, and in the latter year it became a prison. On 15 August 1960, Fort Jesus was declared a national monument.

PEOPLE OF THE COAST

Through the ages, tribes from across Africa have migrated to Kenya, whose east coastline in turn survived turbulent conquests from Arab, Persian and Portuguese quarters. As a result, the tribes around Mombasa are many and various. Mombasa's people are Swahili – a mixture of Arab, Persian and Bantu influences – and the majority are strongly Islamic. From Mombasa northwards to the Sabaki River is the Giriama tribe. Inland from Mombasa are the Duruma, and south are the Digo. North of the Sabaki, along the banks of the Tana River, live the Pokomo, while further north are the Bajun and Somali peoples.

Today, outside the fort's main entrance are two large guns from a more modern time, World War I. They are relics of a battle between two ships, the British *HMS Pegasus* which was sunk by a German cruiser, the *Konigsberg*, in Dar es Salaam Harbour in 1914. The German ship was eventually sunk by the British Navy.

Fort Jesus is popular among tourists and is open to the public daily.

Dhow Trips ⋆⋆⋆

An exciting excursion while staying in Mombasa is to take one of the many dhow trips on offer, particularly those operated by Jahazi Marine Ltd and Tamarind Dhow Safaris (the Tamarind Restaurant, located in both Nairobi and Mombasa, is the best-known seafood eating spot in Kenya). The **Tamarind Dhow** sails twice a day at 12:30 and 18:30, during which one of its legendary seafood meals is served on the open deck; a live band plays for the cruise guests.

Jahazi Marine also operates midday and evening trips. At midday, the dhow sails past Mombasa Old Town and the Old Dhow Harbour where, depending on the time of year, dhows from places as far away as India and the Arabian Gulf may be seen at anchor. Once past the Old Town, the dhow ties up to allow passengers to disembark for an exotic lunch at the gourmet **Harlequin Restaurant**. After lunch, a traditional African herbalist teaches the passengers about African herbs, which can be purchased from him after his talk. Everyone boards the sailing ship once more to head for Tudor Creek and meet the floating market; Africans in traditional dugout canoes approach the dhow to sell carvings, kikois, kangas, baskets and spices. After a lively bartering session, the

Right: *delicious lunchtime seafood fare aboard the Tamarind Dhow out of Mombasa. There is also an evening excursion; a live band entertains passengers.*
Opposite: *exploring Watamu's coral gardens.*

dhow returns to Harlequin Restaurant, from where passengers are transported back to their hotels. On the evening cruise, guests enjoy snacks and drinks to the music of a live band. After just over an hour's cruise, the dhow ties up at the Old Dhow Harbour, where passengers disembark to take a short walk through the Old Town to Fort Jesus. Here they are met by an impressive tableau of men in old costumes holding aloft flaming torches; after a guided tour of the fort, guests enjoy an atmospheric *son et lumière* (sound and light) presentation of Mombasa's history. Finally, a wonderful Portuguese meal is served under the stars in the fort's courtyard.

Both the Tamarind Dhow and Jahazi Marine collect and return all guests to their hotels.

The Coral Reefs ✦✦✦

The endless stretches of beaches to the north and south of Mombasa, lapped by the warm, blue Indian Ocean, ensure this city's continued popularity. From just north of Malindi down to Shimoni in the extreme south, the coast is fringed by a coral reef broken only occasionally in areas occurring opposite a river or creek where fresh water has hindered and killed the growth of the coral. The reef is generally only 640m (700yd) offshore and at low tide it is usually possible to walk across to it.

Snorkelling and scuba diving are popular pursuits along the reef and a number of marine national parks and reserves has been established to protect the underwater life and the wonderful coral. Apart from creating smooth, calm water along the beaches, the reef also keeps out any sharks that could be a menace to bathers. The only hazards that may be encountered are stonefish whose dorsal spines can cause a nasty sting, and sea

MBARAKI PILLAR

As you head straight towards
the Likoni ferry, by turning
right, you will arrive at the
Mbaraki Pillar, a phallic-
like tomb structure built of
coral-rag some time before
1728. It is thought to be the
burial place of the Sheik of
Changamwe who, it is be-
lieved, was the head of one
of the original 12 families living in Mombasa at that time.

urchins whose long-needled spines can be very painful if
stepped upon. The beautiful pebbleless beaches are
white and sandy; seaweed can be washed up on the sand
after storms, otherwise they are remarkably clean.

The coastal climate is governed by two monsoons:
the northeast called the **Kaskazi** blows from December
to March and the southeast, called the **Kusi**, blows
from April to November.

SOUTH COAST

The only way to leave Mombasa Island for the south
coast is via the **Likoni motorized ferry**. Unfortunately, it
is always very busy and delays of at least one hour can
be expected during rush periods. Having been ferried
across, the first in a series of pris-
tine beaches is **Shelly Beach** followed by **Tiwi**, then **Diani**, 35km
(22 miles) south of Mombasa;
Diani is the most popular of all the
beaches. Here, at the Tiwi River
mouth and standing in a grove of
baobab trees is the 18th-century
Kongo Mosque. It is still mostly
intact and is used by the local people as a place of prayer.

Most of the holiday resort
hotels are along Diani Beach,
which is a real tropical paradise of
coconut palms, white sandy
beaches and an opal-blue sea.
Many of the hotels are surrounded
by huge baobabs like those at the
new **Indian Ocean Beach Club**;
one large specimen in the area, its
girth measuring 22m (72ft), is protected by presidential decree. Also
at Diani is the remnant of a once-
large coastal wooded tract, **Jadini
Forest**, which is inhabited by colobus monkeys and other wildlife.

A few miles inland from Diani Beach are the green rolling **Shimba Hills** which rise steeply from the coastal plain up to a height of 457m (1500ft); they are covered mainly with grassland and patches of forest, and offer wonderful views over the surrounding countryside.

The **Shimba Hills National Reserve**, 192km² (74 sq miles), was established in 1968 to protect one of the last breeding herds of sable antelope in Kenya, which were being threatened by the fast-expanding human population. Roan antelope, originally introduced from an area near Thika, north of Nairobi, also occur here, as well as elephant, buffalo, zebra, common waterbuck, lion and leopard. The birdlife is varied; among the more interesting species that can be seen here are the palm-nut vulture, southern-banded snake eagle, grasshopper buzzard, trumpeter and silvery-cheeked hornbill, carmine bee-eater and Fischer's turaco.

Funzi Island ···

Southwards of Diani, all the glitz of modern hotels is soon left behind as the road passes through cashew, coconut and sugar plantations, and the sleepy villages of the Digo people. Approximately 72km (45 miles) from Mombasa is the village of Ramisi. A left turn here leads to the village of Bodo which faces Funzi Island, a private tropical paradise. A short 15-minute boat ride takes you to this delightful hideaway whose only tourists are migrating birds.

A special camp is run by Tony and Robina Duckworth of the **Funzi Island Club**. It is the perfect place for anyone wanting to get away from

> **A CHILLY TALE**
>
> Gazi, a village south of Diani, has a house that once belonged to Sheikh Mbaruk bin Rashid. A local story tells of the sheikh having a special room in the house where he would confine unfaithful wives and disobedient servants, forcing them to inhale burning hot peppers until they saw the error of their ways.

Below: *a weathered rowing boat beached at Diani, some 35km (22 miles) south of Mombasa. Diani, a popular coastal resort area, is noted for its tourist hotels, its palms and giant baobab trees, and for its historic Kongo Mosque.*

Right: *the enchanting Mtwapa Creek, just north of Mombasa. Until fairly recently travellers crossed the water by hand-hauled rope ferry; today they do so over the Japanese-built suspension bridge.*
Opposite: *the pool area of the Flamingo Hotel in Mombasa.*

the crowds. Bird-watching and creek fishing are a speciality, as is the magic of going on a dhow cruise, which often combines a visit to a marine park where guests snorkel or dive, and a superb meal.

Shimoni ***

About 60km (37 miles) along the main road from Mombasa, a sandy turnoff to the left takes you to Shimoni, on the **Pemba Channel**. Meaning 'place of the hole' after an enormous cave which is thought to stretch for 15km (9 miles), Shimoni was once the headquarters of Sir William Mackinnon's Imperial British East Africa. A series of caves, besides the main one, exists; according to legend, slaves were held here until they were transported to Arabia. Some local historians discount this theory, however, claiming they were used by the local people as hiding places when hostile tribes raided the area.

Shimoni is Kenya's deep-sea fishing centre. This sport can be pursued almost all year round except for May, June and sometimes July.

You can also sail on a dhow to the delightful **Wasini** and **Kisite islands**. Some of the best diving and snorkelling in the Indian Ocean is to be experienced here. The islands are dotted around in the Kisite and **Mpunguti** marine national parks and the **Mpunguti National Reserve**, a combined marine area of 21km^2

(8 sq miles). The variety and the colours of the coral and fish are astounding. Most of the divers and snorkellers who join an organized visit to this wonderful spot will enjoy an excellent seafood lunch at the restaurant on Wasini Island. One particular company, Shimoni Aqua Ventures, provides lunch on an uninhabited, secluded island or on board their dhow, the *Pilli Pipa*, while anchored in a remote spot.

NORTH COAST

Leaving Mombasa Island for the north coast by way of the new Nyali Toll Bridge which spans Tudor Creek, the road passes the turn-off for **Freretown**, which was established in 1875 by Sir Bartle Frere as a sanctuary for escaped and emancipated slaves. Just through Freretown is the well-known **Tamarind Restaurant** and the **Krapf Monument**. The monument marks the spot where the first Christian missionary to the area, Dr Krapf, made his pledge to attempt to convert the African continent to Christianity; it is also the burial site of Mrs Krapf and her children. Dr Krapf's wife unfortunately died just four months after arriving in Kenya with her husband.

The road then enters **Nyali**, an elegant suburb and expensive residential area in which the well-known **Nyali Beach Hotel** is situated. Continuing northwards, the road passes the **Bamburi cement work**s. A Swiss ecologist, Rene Haller, was employed by the Bamburi Portland Cement Company to rehabilitate the huge quarries that had been dug by the company over the years, and a wonderful job has certainly been done to hide the quarry scars. Haller has transformed

MAMBA CROCODILE FARM

A popular tourist attraction, Mamba Village has been established near Bamburi, north of Mombasa. *Mamba* means 'crocodile' in Swahili, thus the village is a successful crocodile farm. It is these reptiles – especially when it's feeding time at 17:00 – that most visitors come to see. The village also has a tropical marine aquarium and a botanical garden. Horse and camel riding is on offer, and the popular restaurant serves crocodile meat, zebra, gazelle, buffalo and seafood.

Right: *the ruins of Jumba la Mtwana, or slave master's house, hidden among the trees at the water's edge. The structure, together with the neighbouring mosques, houses and cemetery, was part of a once-flourishing settlement which the Arabs deserted half a millenium ago.*

the area into a wooded wildlife sanctuary containing fish ponds, nature trails and a nonprofit-making farm which is now a major tourist attraction.

The **Mombasa Marine National Park** is situated offshore, and the major concentration of Kenya's coastal hotels occurs along Bamburi Beach.

The road continues northwards over **Mtwapa Creek**, where a number of marinas offers water-skiing and deep-sea fishing. After crossing the creek and turning off immediately to the right, you will find **Kenya Marine Land and Snake Park** (which also organizes dhow trips). Just further on, another road to the right leads to an ancient monument, **Jumba la Mtwana** (slave master's house), which forms part of an ancient city that was abandoned some time between the 14th and 15th centuries. The atmospheric ruins, which have been declared a national monument, are set at the edge of the beach among baobab trees and consist of four mosques (one of which is gently subsiding into the sands), some houses and a cemetery.

Leaving Mtwapa, one passes through farmland, cashew and sisal plantations dotted with huge baobabs. There is a good chance of seeing the most strikingly beautiful of all the bee-eater family, the carmine bee-eater, in this area as it usually perches on the sisal and roadside telephone wires. Yet another coastal hotel area, Kikambala Beach, can be seen on the right. Before arriving at Kilifi, roughly halfway between Mombasa and Malindi, the road passes through territory belonging to the Giriama people, and on through the large Vipingo Sisal Estate.

Kilifi

For many years **Kilifi Creek** was crossed by ferry, which has been replaced with a new toll bridge. Kilifi is best known as the home of the **Mnarani Club**, famous for its big game-fishing competitions; the club can be seen on the right of the road before crossing the new bridge. The creek is a favourite anchorage for ocean-going yachts and is very popular for water-skiing and wind-surfing.

Before crossing the creek, there is a turn-off on the left of the road for the **Mnarani Ruins**, sprawled on a bluff

CARMINE BEE-EATERS

Kilifi Creek is lined with mangrove trees. From November to April they are home to thousands of carmine bee-eaters, which create one of the most incredible sights imaginable as they fly into the trees at sunset to roost, flashing their brilliant plumage. These birds nest in the north of Kenya, in areas close to Lake Turkana, and spend their nonbreeding time along the Kenyan coast where most of them roost (they certainly don't breed, as some travel guides will tell you) in the mangroves of both Kilifi and the nearby Mida Creek.

Left: *printed fabrics in vibrant colours on sale on Jadini Beach along the south coast.*

Above: *fishing craft off Malindi. The port was a major Arab trading centre until the arrival of the Portuguese navigators at the end of the 15th century.*

overlooking the water. The ruins include a group of tombs – one of them a pillar tomb – two mosques and a deep well. They were occupied between the 14th and 17th centuries; pillaged by the warring Galla tribe that swept down from Somalia, the ruined town was only uncovered two centuries later.

Leaving Kilifi, the road passes small, romantic coastal villages shaded by rustling palms, and runs along the edge of the **Arabuko-Sokoke** forest (*see* panel); at one point a glimpse of **Mida Creek** can be seen before arriving at the turn-off for the famous **Gedi Ruins** and the village of **Watamu**.

Watamu

Primarily a small beach resort on **Turtle Bay**, Watamu has on its doorstep its own marine national park. The park and adjacent national reserve, together with the **Malindi Marine National Park and Reserve** (the latter having a combined area of 219km² (84 sq miles) form one of Kenya's biosphere reserves.

The three caves at the entrance to **Mida Creek** are the most attractive feature of the marine park, and are home to a number of giant 1.8m-long (6ft) grouper fish weighing 200kg (440lb). The park wardens protect the caves, limiting the number of visitors to them. Along the beach are a number of hotels, among them **Ocean Sports** and **Hemingways** (famous for their deep-sea fishing).

Mida Creek ✦✦✦

At the southern end of Turtle Bay and guarded by **Whale Island** is the entrance to Mida Creek, mangrove-lined tidal mud flats. Mida is famous for its migrant birds

SOKOKE SCOPS OWL

All of 15cm (6in) high, the Sokoke scops owl is the smallest in Africa – and one of the rarest in the world. It was discovered as recently as 1965. This tiny owl only occurs in Arabuko-Sokoke, where it is unfortunately under pressure due to the threat of deforestation of its restricted habitat. It has a very distinctive call, similar to that of the tinkerbird, which easily identifies it at night.

which concentrate around the creek's food-rich mud from March to April, before flying northwards. Most of the birds are of the sandpiper and plover families, but there is also usually a flock of greater flamingos in residence, adding a splash of colour to this wonderful place. Mida is also the best place to see the unusual and uncommon crab plover, resident here from September to April. Other notable birds are the carmine and Madagascar bee-eaters, and various species of tern. From June to September roseate and bridled terns breed on Whale Island. Most of the Watamu Hotels organize dhow or motorboat trips in the creek, but the best way to see the birds closely is to drive down one of the many sandy tracks off the main Mombasa–Malindi road that lead to the creek's mangrove-fringed shore.

Gedi Ruins ••

Sixteen kilometres (10 miles) south of Malindi, the ruins of an old Arab town set in the midst of the coastal forest combine to provide an atmospheric reminder of the past.

Gedi was founded in the 14th century; it flourished during the late 14th and 15th centuries, but was abandoned in the early 17th century, probably because of increased pressure from the warlike Galla tribe as they moved southwards. The word 'Gedi', or more correctly 'Gede', is a Galla word meaning 'precious'; it is also a personal name. Gedi was originally surrounded by a 2.7m-high (9ft) wall which had at least three gates. The northwest part of the town has been excavated and covers an area of 18ha (44 acres).

Among the excavated ruins are the **Great Mosque**, origin-

A THREATENED FOREST

Parallel to the coast just inland from Malindi and Watamu is the largest remaining stand of indigenous coastal forest in Kenya. Called the Arabuko-Sokoke, this forest reserve covers an area of 372km² (144 sq miles) and is internationally known for its unique endangered bird species, the Sokoke scops owl and Clarke's weaver, and two lesser-known endemic mammals, the Sokoke four-toed mongoose and the golden-rumped elephant shrew. A number of wide drivable tracks enables visitors to travel deep into the forest. Look out for the primitive giant tree ferns. Visitors can call in at the forest station along the Malindi–Mombasa road to arrange for a guide to accompany them.

Below: *the ruins of Gedi, a town founded by Arab traders centuries ago.*

CRUSOE CORDON BLEU

Thirty-three kilometres (21 miles) from Malindi, a turn-off to the right leads down a sandy track to **Robinson Island**, where there is an exciting cordon-bleu seafood restaurant started by a descendant of a Kenyan settler family. Saturated with the atmosphere of a remote desert island, its splendid tropical beauty fulfils all expectations. The island's real name is Kinya'ole, meaning 'barber's island', after a local superstition: local shipbuilder Robinson owned the wells on the isle, and only allowed the local women to collect water once they'd shaven their heads!

ally constructed in the 15th century and rebuilt 100 years later, the **Palace**, the **Dated Tomb** inscribed with its Arabic date AH802 (1399) and the **Pillar Tomb**. A number of wells are now the home of barn owls.

Interesting birds can be seen at Gedi, among them the lizard buzzard, palm-nut vulture, trumpeter hornbill, Narina's trogon and black-breasted glossy starling. Blue monkeys and red-tailed squirrels also live among the ruins. Gedi is administered by The National Museums of Kenya and is open to the public daily from 07:00 to 18:00.

Malindi **

North of Watamu, Kenya's most famous resort town, Malindi, sits in an attractive bay south of the Sabaki River. For centuries Malindi was an important Arab trading centre. Portuguese explorer Vasco da Gama landed here in 1498 and in the following year erected a cross to commemorate the occasion. Carved from Lisbon limestone and inscribed with the Portuguese coat of arms, the cross was originally erected at the site of the Sheikh of Malindi's palace, but was later taken down and re-erected at Vasco da Gama Point.

Malindi became Portugal's most northerly territory in East Africa, reverting to Omani rule during the 17th century, before being taken over by the Galla people.

Nowadays Malindi swarms with foreign tourists, mainly Italians and Germans on package holidays, and there are few signs of those blissfully tranquil former days.

The **Vasco da Gama cross** and **church**, built in 1541, are accessible to the public, and Sheikh Hassan's 15th-century **pillar tomb**, standing beside a 19th-century pillar tomb, can be seen on the waterfront next to the mosque.

Below: *Malindi's Pillar Tomb, which contains the mortal remains of Sheikh Abdul Hassan, and the graceful Jumah Mosque.*

Unfortunately, due to poor farming practices upstream of the Sabaki River, tons of silt are washed into Malindi Bay every year. The beach hotels that were once right on the seashore are now set well back and the silt often stains the once blue water, and is killing the coral in the vicinity of the river. Malindi is a deep-sea fishing centre and the home port of a number of commercial fishing boats.

The Malindi Marine National Park and Reserve, 219km^2 (84 sq miles) in area, extends from Malindi southwards to Watamu. The southern section of the park embraces beautiful coral gardens, and is popular for divers and snorkellers, and visitors in glass-bottomed boats.

LAMU ARCHIPELAGO

An exciting 25-minute flight to the north of Malindi, affording breathtaking views down into a turquoise sea, brings one to the famous Lamu Archipelago, comprising the islands of **Lamu**, **Manda** and **Pate**. The only mode of transport here is the sailboat and charismatic dhow.

> ### BIRDERS' PARADISE
>
> Bird-watchers will not want to miss visiting the mouth of the Sabaki River where, at times, there are thousands of migrant wading birds, including broad-billed sandpipers (the area is the only place in Kenya where this rare migrant is seen regularly). Other special birds found at the mouth of the Sabaki are the Madagascar pratincoles (the Sabaki is virtually the only place other than Madagascar where they can be seen); the rare and localized Malindi pipit too can be spotted – with diligence – in the sand dunes along the river banks.

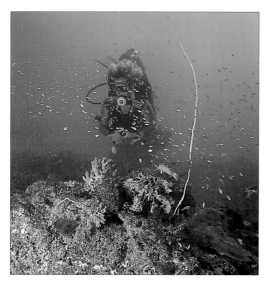

Left: *the coral reefs offshore of Malindi and the Lamu Archipelago to the north serve as a mecca for scuba divers and snorkellers. Visitors can also experience trips in a glass-bottomed boat.*

Lamu Island ✱✱✱

No matter whether one arrives by road or by air, the only way to get to 19km-long (12 miles) Lamu Island is by diesel-powered dhow. Visitors arriving by air land on **Manda Island**; a five-minute walk takes them to **Mkandi Channel**, where they can cross the strait aboard a dhow to Lamu Town or on to **Peponi's Hotel**. Those arriving by road will have to leave their vehicles on the mainland at **Mokowe** and take a dhow from the town's jetty.

Visiting Lamu Town is a journey back in time; here life goes on much as it has done for hundreds of years. The town itself has been in existence since at least the 9th century, although most of its dwellings date from the 19th century. In the 1500s Lamu was a thriving port exporting slaves, ivory, rhino horn and mangrove poles. Now, except for the continued export of a few mangrove poles, its main business is tourism.

The town is a maze of narrow streets and small flower-filled courtyards enclosed by walls, its houses made of coral rag, many of which feature ornately carved wooden doors and lintels. Most of the streets remain undisturbed by motor vehicles, as donkeys alone find enough room to navigate them. There is only one vehicle on Lamu Island, owned by the district governor.

The people of Lamu are orthodox Muslims and wear the traditional white *kanzu* and an embroidered cap (*kofia*); women wear brightly coloured *khangas* but cover up in a black cloth, called a *bui-bui*, when they go outdoors. Of Lamu's mosques, none is remarkable as each differs little in appearance from nearby homes.

The **Old Fort**, built by the Omani Arabs in 1812 and until recently a prison, is worth a visit; so is the museum. Otherwise the visitor can soak up the atmosphere by taking a slow stroll through the streets. The museum was

---

TROPICAL ISLAND PARADISE

Northeast of Pate Island, the Kiunga Marine Reserve stretches from the Somali border down to Oseni; adjacent to this coastal village lies Kiwaiyu Island, a long, narrow, strip of sand. Kenya's most exclusive and expensive getaway, Kiwaiyu Lodge, is situated on the mainland in a beautiful bay opposite the island's northern tip. The lodge (if one can call it that) consists of a few small thatch-built chalets perched on the beach. All types of watersports are on offer (sailing, water-skiing, diving) and the food is legendary. Kiwaiyu Lodge is accessible only by air or boat.

once the home of the British district officer and has many interesting exhibits, among them the reconstruction of a traditional Swahili home, and models of various types of dhow and canoe. There are also some very good displays of carved wooden doors, and two examples of carved ivory *siwas* – wind instruments which are still used today on special occasions such as the Maulidi celebration (this takes place after the Prophet's birthday).

The village of **Shela** is a 40-minute walk along the shore. Popular among visitors to Lamu Island, the village has a lovely dune-lined beach. The interesting **Friday Mosque** in the village has a rocket-like tower.

Manda Island **

Close to Lamu, across the narrow Mkandi Channel, is the mystery-shrouded Manda Island with its extensive ruins of the old Swahili city, **Takwa**, which flourished between the 15th and 17th centuries before being inexplicably abandoned. The ruins sprawl over an area of 5ha (12 acres) and include a tomb dated 1681. All of the buildings and the mosque face north towards Mecca.

Pate Island **

A two-hour boat ride to the north of Manda Island takes one to Pate Island, which has some of the most impressive ruins in Kenya. Among these is the recently excavated Shanga, an ancient Swahili city state that is at least 1200 years old. The ruins cover an area of 8ha (20 acres), and were uncovered with the help of members of the Operation Drake Team.

> **MAULIDI CELEBRATION**
>
> All of Lamu's mosques participate in this Muslim celebration (the exact date varies so it is best to check with the Lamu Museum), which continues for several days each year. Sheikh Habib Salih, Lamu's patron during the late 19th century, brought fame to the small town for introducing the prophet's birthday celebration and turning the occasion into a major annual festival. Muslims from across East Africa are drawn to these festivities, which include singing and dancing.

Opposite: *an elegant dhow sets out from Lamu Island.*
Below: *the Dhow Palace Hotel on Lamu.*

The Coral Coast at a Glance

The prime time for fishermen, snorkellers and scuba divers is **August to March** when seas are calm and the water clear. Over April and May, and into June, many hotels close, but visitors are sure to find a hotel open during that time.

Major **car-hire** companies are represented at Moi International Airport, and at most bigger coastal hotels. The best way to get to Lamu is **by air** from Mombasa or Malindi, contact Malindi Air Services, tel: (011) 433061, fax: 434264, or Safari Air Services/Prestige Air Services, tel: (011) 433059, fax: 226157. They also offer visits by air (one- or two-day excursions) to national parks and reserves. Visits to Tsavo National Park and Shimba Hills National Reserve can be arranged through **Galu Safaris**, tel: (011) 471465, and other safari companies.

Mombasa Town
Castle Hotel, Moi Ave: tel: (011) 21683.
Manor Hotel, Nyerere Ave: tel: (011) 31643.
New Outrigger Hotel, Ras Liwatoni: tel: (011) 20822.

South Coast
Shimba Hills Lodge in Shimba National Reserve: tree top game-viewing lodge, book through Block Hotels.

Indian Ocean Beach Club: new hotel resembling Swahili village, on Diani Beach, book through Block Hotels.
Diani House: secluded home, book through Bush Homes of East Africa.
Jadini Beach Hotel: one of original beach hotels, book through Alliance Hotels.
Chale Island, 12km (7 miles) south of Diani Beach: 25 luxury bungalows and tents on the beach, write to Chale Paradise Island, PO Box 4, Ukunda; tel: (0127) 2127, fax: 3319/20.
The Samawati House, Msambweni Beach: Arab-style house with sweeping beach-front, book through Safaris Unlimited (Africa).
Funzi Island Club, 72km (45 miles) south of Mombasa: luxury camp set on secluded island, birdlife superb, call Sargas, tel: (02) 212763 (Nairobi) or tel: (0127) 317179 (Diani), fax: 2396.
Pemba Channel Inn, Pemba Channel: mainly for fishermen as no beach here, but ideal base for visits to nearby marine national park and reserve; contact Pemba Channel Fishing Club Ltd, tel: (011) 313749, fax: 316875.

North Coast
Tamarind Village, Nyali: fully equipped, self-catering or room service, write to The Tamarind Village, PO Box 95805, Mombasa; tel: (011) 471729, fax: 472106.
Nyali Beach Hotel: book

through Block Hotels.
Mombasa Beach Hotel, Nyali: write to PO Box 90414, Mombasa; tel: (011) 471861.
Whitesands, Bamburi Beach: book through Sarova Hotels.
Severin Sea Lodge, Bamburi Beach: write to PO Box 90173, Mombasa; tel: (011) 485001.
Serena Beach Hotel, Shanzu Beach: built in style of Swahili village, contact Serena Hotels.

Kilifi
Takaungu House: on beach, for six guests, book through Bush Homes of East Africa.
Mnarani Club: owned by African Safari Club chain, write to PO Box 81443, Kilifi.

Watamu
Hemingways: highly recommended, write to PO Box 267, Watamu; tel: (0122) 32624, fax: 32256.
Turtle Bay Beach Hotel: write to PO Box 22309, Nairobi; tel: (02) 221143, fax: 217261.
Ocean Sports: write to PO Box 100, Watamu; tel: (0122) 32008, fax: 32266.

Malindi
Indian Ocean Lodge: book through Safcon Travel.
Che-Shale, 20km (12 miles) north of Malindi: small super-luxury lodge among sand dunes: write to PO Box 857, Malindi; tel: (0123) 20676.

Lamu Archipelago
Lamu Palace Hotel, on waterfront: all rooms air-conditioned, write to the hotel

The Coral Coast at a Glance

at PO Box 86, Lamu; tel: (0121) 33272.
Petley's Inn in Lamu town: first hotel on the island, write to PO Box 4, Lamu; tel: (0121) 33107.
Peponi Hotel, Shela village: at water's edge; write to PO Box 24, Lamu; tel: (0121) 33421/23, fax: 33029.
Blue Safari Club, Manda Island: small *bandas* on beach (excellent), write to Bruno Brighetti's Blue Safari Club, PO Box 41759, Nairobi; tel: (02) 338838, fax: 218939.
Kiwaiyu Safari Village, Kiwaiyu: very exclusive, Kenya's top beach accommodation, write to PO Box 55343, Nairobi; tel: (02) 503030, fax: 503149.

WHERE TO EAT

Dhow lunch cruise (on *Pilli Pipa*) or a five-course meal on a 'desert' island, very highly recommended, call **Shimoni Aqua Ventures**, ask for Shimoni 8.
Tamarind Restaurant, Mombasa: Moorish-styled seafood restaurant overlooking Mombasa Old Harbour; dhow offers lunch or dinner cruises, tel: (011) 471747, fax: 472106.
Hemingways, highly recommended, tel: (0122) 32624.
Le Pichet, north of Nyali bridge: French gourmet cuisine, tel: (011) 485465/923.
Ali Barbour's, popular seafood restaurant set in coral cave on Diani Beach, tel: (0127) 2163 or 2033.

Wasini Island Restaurant: beach seafood restaurant, dhow cruises stop here for lunch; reservations at Wasini Island booking office in Jadini Beach Hotel, tel: (0127) 2331, fax: 3154.
Driftwood Beachclub in Malindi, international and seafood cuisine, tel: (0123) 20155 or 20406.

ACTIVITIES AND EXCURSIONS

Deep-sea fishing: Hemingways, Watamu, tel: (0122) 32624; Kingfisher Lodge, Malindi, tel: (0123) 21168; Hall Mark Charters, Mtwapa Creek, tel: (011) 485680; Pat Hemphill's Sea Adventures, tel: Shimoni 12 or 13; Pemba Channel Fishing Club, Mombasa, tel: (011) 313749.
Diving: Shimoni Aqua Ventures, tel: Shimoni 8; Tiwi Scuba Divers, Divebase at Minilets, tel: (0127) 51059; Ocean Sports Hotel, Watamu, tel: (0122) 32008.
Dhow cruises: Shimoni Aqua Ventures, tel: Shimoni 8; Kisiti Dhow Tours (lunch at Wasini Island), tel: (0126) 12331; Tamarind, Mombasa, tel: (011) 471747; Ocean Sports, Watamu, tel: (0122) 32008; Peponi Hotel, Lamu, tel: (0121) 33154; Jahazi Marine

Ltd, Mombasa, tel: (011) 472213.

USEFUL ADDRESSES

Safari companies
Galu Safaris Ltd, tel: (0123) 20493 (Malindi), or tel: (011) 471465 (Mombasa).
Kingfisher Safaris, tel: (0123) 21168 (Malindi).
Pollman's Tours and Safaris, tel: (011) 312565/6/7 (Mombasa), fax: 312245.
Southern Cross Safaris, tel: (011) 20737 (Mombasa).

Booking agencies
Alliance Hotels Ltd, PO Box 49839, Nairobi; tel: (02) 337501, fax: 219212.
Block Hotels, PO Box 47557, Nairobi; tel: (02) 335807, fax: 340541.
Bush Homes of East Africa Ltd, PO Box 56923, Nairobi; tel: (02) 506139, fax: 502739.
Safaris Unlimited (Africa) Ltd, PO Box 24181, Nairobi; tel: (02) 891168, fax: 891113.
Safcon Travel, PO Box 59224, Nairobi; tel: (02) 503265, fax: 506824.
Sarova Hotels, PO Box 30680, Nairobi; tel: (02) 333248, fax: 211472.
Serena Hotels, PO Box 48690, Nairobi; tel: (02) 710511, fax: 718103.

MOMBASA	J	F	M	A	M	J	J	A	S	O	N	D
AVERAGE TEMP. °F	81	82	82	81	79	77	75	75	77	79	81	82
AVERAGE TEMP. °C	27	28	28	27	26	25	24	24	25	26	27	28
Hours of Sun Daily	8	9	9	7	6	7	7	8	8	9	9	8
RAINFALL in	1	0	1	4	6	2	1	2	2	2	3	1
RAINFALL mm	18	10	29	109	150	53	35	48	45	62	64	33
Days of Rainfall	11	1	2	11	15	13	12	8	9	8	7	6

Travel Tips

Tourist information

The Kenya Tourist Board has offices in various countries: the United Kingdom (London), the United States (New York and Beverly Hills), France (Paris), Germany (Frankfurt), Hong Kong, Japan (Tokyo), Sweden (Stockholm) and Switzerland (Zürich). There are also tourist information offices in Mombasa on Moi Avenue, tel: (011) 3123, and in Malindi on Lamu Road.

Safari companies: There are many safari companies in Kenya whose price and service vary tremendously. You are advised to use only ones that are members of KATO (Kenya Association of Tour Operators). If in doubt, do not hesitate to contact the KATO Office, 3rd floor, Jubilee Insurance Exchange, Mama Ngina Street, Nairobi, tel: (02) 25570, fax: (02) 28402.

Entry documents

Every visitor has to be in possession of a valid passport; visa requirements vary from time to time, so you are strongly advised to check the latest requirements at the airline or the nearest Kenya Tourist Board Office, Embassy or High Commission. Visitors with a valid passport may obtain a visitor's pass on arrival if in possession of an onward or return airline ticket. A visitor's pass is normally valid for three months.

Customs

Although there is no import duty on photographic equipment, you may be asked to pay. If asked, refuse and request a senior official. You may also be asked to record the serial numbers of your cameras, lens and video camera in your passport – this is a valid requirement.

When leaving the country, travellers are required to report to the customs desk before checking in, where you will be asked the contents of your baggage. The export of rhino horn, ivory and any wildlife items is strictly illegal.

Departure Tax

On all departures from Kenya, an airport tax of US$20 per person is payable in foreign currency. Other currencies are acceptable, but not Kenyan shillings. It is much more convenient if you have the exact amount of US dollars, as change is often a problem. There is also a departure tax of Kshs100 charged on all internal flights departing from government airports.

Health requirements

Visitors who are from, or who have recently passed through, a yellow-fever zone, must be able to produce a valid international certificate of vaccination. Rules regarding health requirements change regularly; when planning your trip, therefore, it is advisable to check with your airline for the latest information.

Air Travel

The major points of entry into Kenya are Jomo Kenyatta International Airport (JKIA) in Nairobi and Moi International Airport in Mombasa. Wilson Airport is the main airport for charter services. Kenya Airways is Africa's fastest growing airline and operates a fleet of modern aircraft.

Kenya Airways
Flight information and reservations:
Nairobi: tel: (02) 29291 or 82288/171;
Mombasa: tel: (02) 43400;
Kisumu: tel: (035) 4056;
Malindi: tel: (0123) 2192.

Road Travel

Kenya has an extensive and well-signposted road network – 8300km (5157 miles) are bitumen and 54,000km (33,555 miles) are earth and gravel. The state of the road surfaces is variable, from well maintained to extremely neglected and potholed. The roads in the national park are generally good murram (laterite) surfaces.

In Kenya one drives on the left. The general speed limit is 100kph (60mph) on highways and 50kph (30mph) in towns and villages. Drivers require a valid driving licence which ought to be carried at all times. Visitors may use their domestic licences for up to 90 days, providing that they are fully endorsed at the Road Transport Office in Nyayo House, Nairobi.
Car hire: There are numerous car-hire companies, but the most well known are:
Kenya Rent a Car (Avis):
Nairobi, tel: (02) 36794;
JKIA, tel: (02) 82186;
Mombasa, tel: (011) 2048;
Malindi, tel: (0123) 2513.
Hertz UTC:
Nairobi, tel: (02) 31960;
Mombasa, tel: (011) 36333/4;
Malindi, tel: (0123) 2040.
Insurance: Your vehicle must be covered by a third party

insurance policy; if you are hiring a car the rental firm is responsible for making the appropriate arrangements.
Maps: Regional and city maps are available from bookshops. Both Nation Bookshop and Prestige Booksellers in Nairobi have good selections.
Petrol: Cities, towns and main routes are well served by filling stations. In main towns there is a 24-hour service, other stations are open from 06:00 until 18:00. All fuel – super, regular or diesel – is sold in litres. There is no octane rating shown on pumps. Pump attendants see to your needs as there is no self-service in Kenya. Always check that the pump is zeroed prior to filling up.
Automobile Association:
Situated at Hurlingham Shopping Centre, PO Box 40087, Nairobi; tel: (02) 70382/3; emergency service, tel: (02) 73195.
Coach travel: This form of travel (between Nairobi and Mombasa) is for the younger or hardier traveller, and not recommended for the faint-hearted. Do not accept any sweets or other food from fellow travellers as there have been many cases of travellers being drugged and robbed.

Rail Travel

Rail travel is a comfortable and relatively inexpensive method of travel. On a daily basis, Kenya Railways operates services to Mombasa and Kisumu. Each evening two trains leave Nairobi for the 12-hour journey to Mombasa.

First-, second- and third-class tickets are available. First class consists of two-berth compartments with fold-away bunk beds and a washbasin. Second class is similar but has four-berth compartments with fold-away bunk beds, while third class has seats only. Bedding is available at a small extra cost. There is a dining car offering dinner and breakfast at very reasonable prices. For first and second class it is advisable to book a few days in advance; this can be done through a travel agent or directly at the station. Kenya Railways, enquiries and reservations:
Nairobi, tel: (02) 221211;
Mombasa, tel: (011) 31222;
Kisumu, tel: (035) 42211.

Boat Travel

Lake steamers: Kenya Railways operates ferries that connect Kisumu with Kendu Bay, Homa Bay, Mfangano Island and Mbita Point, tel: (035) 42271.
Dhows: It is possible to travel by dhow from Mombasa to Malindi and Lamu, and it is also possible to travel by dhow to Dar es Salaam and the islands of Pemba. There is no set schedule and the visitor must enquire on the spot.

Money Matters

The Kenyan currency unit is the shilling, which is divided into 100 cents. Coins are issued in denominations of 5, 10 and 50 cents and 1 and 5 shillings. Notes are issued in denominations of 5, 10, 20, 50, 100, 200 and 500 shillings. Foreign currency regulations are being slowly revised; at the time of writing foreign currency does not have to be declared on arrival or departure. The importation and exportation of Kenyan currency is not allowed. All foreign currency must be exchanged at banks or licensed exchange facilities such as major hotels and safari lodges. On arrival in Nairobi or Mombasa visitors are advised to change the bulk of their foreign currency or traveller's cheques at the airport or at the hotel. Safari lodges often have a shortage of cash, so queueing and long delays waiting for cash are very often the case. Banks in towns other than Nairobi or Mombasa will change foreign currency and traveller's cheques but are very slow – 45 minutes or more is not at all unusual – which can make you somewhat unpopular with your fellow travellers. Do not be tempted by blackmarket dealers who are prevalent in Nairobi streets.

Banks operate a 24-hour service at Jomo Kenyatta International Airport in Nairobi and at Moi International Airport in Mombasa. Banking hours in the bigger cities and towns are: 09:00 to 15:00 Monday to Friday, and 09:00 to 11:00 on Saturdays. Traveller's cheques accepted at hotels, lodges, restaurants and shops, including roadside curio dealers. However, they are not usually accepted at the smaller places such as petrol service stations.

Value Added Tax: VAT of 18% is levied on most goods and services, and cannot be reclaimed by visitors.

Tipping: Tipping is usual to those giving a good service. Ten per cent is acceptable at hotels and restaurants even though there is frequently a service charge on your bill. There is also a training levy on restaurant bills. It is usual to tip your tour driver or guide, at least Kshs100 per day.

Measurements

Kenya uses the metric system.

Accommodation

Although there is a grading system ranging from one to five stars it is seldom used. The best hotels in Nairobi, the best beach hotels at the coast and the top safari lodges are of international standard. Major groups are Serena Hotels, Sarova Hotels, Hilton Hotels, Block Hotels, Lonrho Hotels and Musiara Ltd. Many ranches and private homes will accept visitors; these are highly recommended for those who are interested in something different or who would like to get away from the crowds. In a number of the national parks there is self-catering accommodation. This tends to be very basic and the visitor is advised to take food and bedding, crockery, cutlery and cooking utensils as well as a stove; although cooking gas and bedding should be available, they often are not. Make sure that you are well prepared, as national parks' rules forbid you to drive to the nearest lodge for food and drinks after dark. (Ol Tukai Lodge in Amboseli is possibly the only exception but check on arrival if you intend to visit the nearby Amboseli Lodge.)

Clothes: What to Pack

Kenya enjoys warm to hot dry seasons and cool to chilly rainy seasons. Nights can be surprisingly cold, especially in the highland areas. Dress is informal, although after dark 'smart casual' is worn. Some restaurants do not allow blue-jeans in the evening and a few require jacket and tie for gentlemen and a similar standard of dress for ladies. Mount Kenya Safari Club

CONVERSION CHART		
FROM	**TO**	**MULTIPLY BY**
Millimetres	Inches	0.0394
Metres	Yards	1.0936
Metres	Feet	3.281
Kilometres	Miles	0.6214
Hectares	Acres	2.471
Litres	Pints	1.760
Kilograms	Pounds	2.205
Tonnes	Tons	0.984
To convert Celsius to Fahrenheit: x 9 ÷ 5 + 32		

requires jacket and tie for gentlemen, and ladies are not allowed to wear trousers in the evening, except for traditional costume. Casual wear is usual at the coast and on safari in the game parks. Beach wear is only to be worn at the pool or beach. Please note that nude bathing is not allowed and any offender will be prosecuted. Year-round clothing should be quite lightweight and a hat is a must. A light jacket is necessary all year round, and a warm sweater is advisable for the months of the cool season – June to August.

Business Hours

Businesses generally operate from 09:00 to 17:00 Monday to Friday with a break for one hour at lunch time, usually from 13:00 to 14:00. Some businesses, such as travel agencies, are open on Saturdays from 09:00 to 13:00. Most shops and stores will not open for business until 09:00 but will remain open over the lunch hour and close at 17:00. Some of the larger supermarkets and modern shopping complexes remain open at weekends and on public holidays. In Mombasa some businesses open at 07:00 but may close between 12:30 and15:30 or 16:00. However, they will remain open until well after dark. City bars and nightclubs remain open until 03:00.

Telephones

The country code is 254. International and local direct dialling is available from Nairobi and Mombasa and most other towns in Kenya. Telephone directories list the dialling codes. If you have any telephone enquiries, dial 991 for assistance.

Facsimile transmission: Facilities are available in most larger hotels and also in some safari lodges. Be warned that hotels and lodges make a heavy surcharge for telephone and fax service.

Electricity

The power system is 240 volts AC. Plugs are usually 13-amp square pins. The bedrooms in all the larger hotels and lodges are equipped with electrical outlet sockets, and

---

PUBLIC HOLIDAYS

New Year's Day 1 January
Good Friday
Easter Monday
Labour Day 1 May
Madaraka Day 1 June
(anniversary of self-government)
Idd ul Fitr, a Muslim holiday timed for the sighting of the new moon after Ramadan (this holiday is taken by both the Muslim and non-Muslim communities)
Nyayo Day 10 October
Kenyatta Day (Kenyatta's birthday) 20 October
Jamhuri (Independence Day) 12 December
Christmas Day 25 December
Boxing Day 26 December
Those holidays falling on a Sunday include the following Monday as a public holiday.

---

even smaller hotels are able and willing to recharge guest's video camera batteries in the reception area.

Time

Kenya is three hours ahead of Greenwich Mean Time (GMT).

Medical Services

Visitors are responsible for their own medical arrange-ments and are advised to take out medical insurance before departure. Nairobi and Mombasa have several good private hospitals. There are also a number of physicians and surgeons of international reputation. Good dentists and opticians are also available. Visitors can have temporary membership of the Flying Doctor Service, as, in the event of an accident or illness, emergency evacuation to Nairobi may be necessary. There are also some private insurance companies who will evacuate visitors (check with your safari company for details). The African Medical & Research Foundation (AMREF) has a flying doctor service, the telephone number of which is (02) 501301; emergency numbers are: (02) 501280/ 997/331 and 336886. The African Air Rescue is a private company with which you can buy temporary membership for US$50 for 30 days' coverage, tel: (02) 337306/ 504/030 and 215758/759.

There are many chemists or drugstores in Nairobi and Mombasa, staffed by well-qualified pharmacists. Most drugs are available but often listed under a different brand name. Although most chemists are closed over weekends and during public holidays, there is always one open at these times. The name of the chemist open is usually posted on the door of those that are closed, or it can be obtained from the local hospital. Visitors who are taking regular medication should ensure they bring an adequate supply of their drugs with them.

Health Hazards

Malaria: All visitors to Kenya should be taking anti-malarial prophylactics on arrival in the country, throughout their stay and for a designated time after leaving as malaria is endemic in most areas of Kenya. It is important that these tablets are taken between 18:00 and 19:00 and not in the morning. Some people find that they have to take their anti-malarial tablets with a meal, otherwise they feel unwell. Avoidance of the malaria-carrying mosquito is also very important. As it usually feeds after dark, from about 21:00 onwards, the following is suggested: always sleep under a mosquito net if one is provided; wear long clothing after dark, keeping the ankles covered; and make use of mosquito repellents. (This advice is especially important to remember when sitting around the traditional safari camp fire.) When leaving your room or tent after dark do not leave any lights on inside. However, whatever

you do, you may still contract malaria. At the first sign of illness, consult a doctor (this is particularly important if you fall ill after you have returned home), making it known that you have been in a malaria area. Insist that a blood test be taken. Early diagnosis and treatment will result in your being cured.

Bilharzia: Also known as schistosomiasis, bilharzia is a debilitating waterborne disease caused by a parasitical worm. The worm lives in a small water snail which is usually found in shallow water along the edges of lakes, dams and slow-moving rivers and streams. Bilharzia is not known to occur in either Lake Naivasha or in the area adjacent to the three tourist resorts on Lake Victoria. Before swimming in any water be sure to ask whether it is free of bilharzia.

Aids: The risk of contracting Aids is no greater in Kenya than elsewhere, providing that the usual, well-publicized precautions are taken.

Creepy crawlies: Although snakes, scorpions and spiders are certainly not uncommon in Kenya, they are seldom seen. Even so, when visiting the toilet at night it is still advisable to wear shoes, and where there is no electrical power to use a torch to ensure that you are not about to step on anything nasty! When walking in the bush avoid long grass whenever possible, wear long pants or apply a liberal amount of insect repellent for protection

against ticks. Although ticks in Kenya do not carry Lyme disease, there is still a very slight chance of contracting tick fever.

Drinking water: Most hotels and lodges provide flasks of filtered and boiled water in their guest rooms. Bottled water is available from most hotels and lodges but is expensive. If possible, buy it at a supermarket in Nairobi or Mombasa or at a *duka* (shop) in a small town that you may pass through on your way to the wildlife areas.

Emergencies

The national emergency telephone number is 999 or 0 for operator assistance. Although there is no reliable national ambulance service, there are a number of private ambulance services for insured people. Cover can be bought before commencing your safari and, of course, there is also the Flying Doctor Service. Some safari companies enlist their clients in temporary membership of the service. Almost all safari lodges and camps are in radio contact with the Flying Doctor Service at their base in Nairobi.

Security

Nairobi and Mombasa are as safe for visitors as any major city or town in the world. Avoid deserted streets and beaches, especially if you are alone, and at night take a taxi if you need to leave your hotel. Do not wear expensive-looking jewellery or watches and if possible do not carry a handbag which could easily be snatched. In other words, take the same precautions that you would in any other city in the world. Do not leave valuables or cash and traveller's cheques in your room or tent.

The con man is perhaps a bigger danger to the tourist than actual theft. The con man will often pose as a student refugee from one of Kenya's neighbouring countries, usually one that has featured in the international news recently. When staying at a wildlife lodge or camp, do not wander off into the bush alone, keep to the clearly marked paths. Buffalo and elephant have become very tame in the vicinity of many lodges and camps and can be dangerous if suddenly disturbed. At night many lodges and camps provide *askaris* (guards) to escort you to and from your room or tent; make use of them and do not be foolhardy.

Photography

Although Kenya is famous for being a land of photographic opportunities you must not attempt to photograph subjects such as the president, military installations, military personnel in uniform, police, prisons and prisoners. Remember that you should never photograph people without first asking their permission – Muslim women in traditional dress often dislike being photographed and Maasai and Samburu

warriors will expect to be recompensed for posing.

Film, both slide film and colour negative film, is widely available in Nairobi and Mombasa and in almost all safari lodges and camps. It is much cheaper in Nairobi – Expo Camera Centre on Mama Ngina Street is the cheapest. Camera batteries and video cassettes, on the other hand, are not readily available from the camps and so it is advisable to stock up in Nairobi or Mombasa.

Still photography: Two lenses are all that is needed for most wildlife photography, the exception being bird photography. A 28mm to 85mm lens is adequate for photographing scenery and people, and a 100mm to 300mm lens is ideal for taking general wildlife photographs. For bird photography, on the other hand, a lens of 400mm or more is required, especially for close-up photographs. There is often a temptation to make use of x2 extenders to double the magnification of the lens. Be warned that this makes focusing more difficult. However, certain camera manufacturers such as Canon and Nikon produce a x1.4 extender, which, when used on a fixed 300mm or 400mm lens, can result in excellent photographs.

The really enthusiastic photographer is advised to bring two camera bodies. Not only is the second body useful if you come across problems but it can also be loaded with a higher speed film for those

difficult shots either early in the morning or late in the afternoon. For high quality photography, slow film such as 50ASA, 64ASA or 100ASA should always be used. It is also a good idea to fit a filter on the front of any lens to circumvent the dust problem. Use a small tripod that can rest on the vehicle's roof, or a beanbag to help to keep the camera steady. To avoid missing any good shots, always keep your camera ready to use and not zipped up in your camera bag. It is a good idea to have the camera switched on, resting on your knee and covered with a towel or kikoi.

Video photography: More and more visitors nowadays prefer using video cameras to still or movie cameras. Rather than freely moving the camera around, rest it on the vehicle's window-frame or roof, using a beanbag to keep it steady. Better results will be obtained by letting the subject move into or out of the viewfinder as opposed to following it as it moves. Do not take photographs out of the roof hatch – keep the camera angle as low as possible. Don't forget to use your video camera at night as some spectacular footage can be obtained.

Sound can either enhance or spoil the final result. Wind is perhaps the biggest problem, followed by chat from your safari companions. A special directional microphone fitted with a good wind cover is the answer to this problem.

INDEX

Aberdare National Park **41**
alkaline lakes **68**
Amboseli National Park **92**
animals
  big five **13**
  colobus monkey **40**
  elephants,Tsavo **97**
  gerenuk **81**
  Grevy's zebra **85**
  sitatunga **58**
Arabuko-Sokoke Forest 10, 114, **115**
Arap Moi, Daniel **24**
Ark, The 42, 44, 45, 47
Baden-Powell, Lord **42**
balloon safaris **51**
birds **14**
  carmine bee-eater **113**
  flamingos **70, 75**
  Sokoke scops owl **114**
  sunbirds **15**
bird-watching 14, **117**
Bomas of Kenya **39**
camel safaris 45, **82**
Central Island National Park 64
Chaimu Crater 96
Chania Falls 40, 41
Chyulu Hills National Park 94
climate **9**, 33, 49, 61, 79, 91, 103
conservation **12, 13**
coral reefs **107**
deep-sea fishing **110**
dhow trips **106**
drink **31**
Eburru 71
economy **25 – 27**
education **27**
fishing **67**
food **31**
Fourteen Falls 40
Funzi Island **109**
Gedi ruins **115**
Giraffe Manor **38**
golf courses **30**
government **25 – 27**
Great Rift Valley **61, 62**
Happy Valley **72**
health services **27**
history **16 – 25**
Homa Bay **54**
horseback safaris 45
infrastructure 26

Jumba la Mtwana 112
Kakamega Forest 11, 14
Kapenguria 58
Karen Blixen Museum **38**
Kariandusi 71
Kenya Marineland and Safari Park 112
Kenyatta, Jomo **22**
Kericho **56**
Kiambethu Tea Estate 39
Kilifi **113**
Kinangop 41
Kisite Island 110
Kisite Marine National Park 110
Koobi Fora 16
Kora National Reserve **86**
Krapf Monument 111
Laikipia National Reserve 44
Laikipia Plateau 44
Lake Baringo 15, 66
Lake Bogoria **68**
Lake Elmenteita **71**
Lake Jipe 97
Lake Logipe 65
Lake Magadi 62, **74**
Lake Naivasha 62, **73**
Lake Nakuru **69**
Lake Turkana **62**
Lake Victoria 51, **54**
Lamu Archipelago **117**
Lamu Island **118**
  Old Fort 118
language **29**
  Swahili **17, 29**
Leakey, Dr Richard 14
Lewa Wildlife Conservancy **83**
Limuru Uplands **39**
Lugard's Falls 8, 98
Malindi **116**
Malindi Marine National Park and Reserve 114, 117
Mamba Crocodile Farm **111**
Manda Island **119**
Maralal Game Sanctuary **88**
Marsabit Mountain 7
Marsabit National Park and Reserve **87**
Masai Mara National Reserve **50**
matatus **27**
Mau Escarpment 49
Mau Mau **23**
Mbaraki Pillar **108**

Meru National Park **84**
Mfangano Island Camp 55
Mida Creek **114**
Mnarani Ruins 113
Molo River Safari **66**
Mombasa Marine National Park 112
Mombasa Town 103
  Fort Jesus **105**
  Government Square 104
  Mandhry Mosque 104
  Old Harbour, 107
  Old Mombasa Town **104**
  shopping **106**
Mountain Lodge 44, 47
Mount Elgon **57**
Mount Kenya 15, **43**
Mount Kenya National Park 41, **43**
Mount Kenya safari lodges **44**
Mount Kilimanjaro **94**
Mount Kulal 65
Mount Longonot **73**
Mpunguti National Reserve 110
Mtwapa Creek 112
Mudanda Rock 98
Mzima Springs 95
Nabuyatom Cone 65
Nairobi **34**
  Kenyatta Conference Centre 34
  Nairobi Animal Orphanage **37**
  Nairobi Arboretum Forest Reserve **36**
  Nairobi National Park 33, **36**
  National Museum **34**
  Railway Museum **35**
  Wildlife Education Centre 37
National Assembly **25**
Ndere Island National Park 55
Ngare Sergoi Rhino Sanctuary 83
Ngulia **96**
Ngulia Mountain 97
north coast **111**
Observation Hill 92, 93
Ol Doinyo Sabuk National Park **40**
Ol Doinyo Satima 41
Ol Tukai 92
Ostrich Park 38

Pate Island **119**
people **16**, 28 – 30
  coastal **105**
  el-Molo **63**
  Galla **17**
  Kikuyu 23
  Luhya 49, 56
  Luo 23, 49, 54
  Maasai **52**
  Njemps **67**
recreation **30**
religion **29**
Rift Valley volcanoes 69
Roaring Rocks 96
Saiwa Swamp National Park **58**
Samburu-Buffalo Springs Reserve 15, **80**
Shaba National Reserve **82**
Sheldrick, Daphne 37
Shimba Hills National Reserve 109
Shimoni **110**
Sibiloi National Park **63**
soapstone **55**
south coast **108**
Soysambu Wildlife Sanctuary 70
sport **30**
Taita Hills **99**
Takwa 119
Tana River National Reserve **87**
Teleki's Volcano 65,
Thika **39**
Thomson, Joseph **18**
Treetops 42, 44, 47
Tsavo East National Park **97**
Tsavo National Park **94**
Tsavo West National Park **95**
Turtle Bay 114
Uganda railway **20**
Utamaduni 38
vegetation **10, 57**
  baobab **98**
  Cape chestnut **37**
  doum palm **84**
  flowers 82
volcanic islands, Turkana **64**
volcanoes, Rift Valley **69**
walking safaris 45
Wasini Islands 110
Watamu **114**
waterfalls **41**
wealth 26
Yatta Plateau 95